HOLT SCIENCE & TECHNOLOGY

Life Science

DIRECTED READING
WORKSHEETS

This book was printed with soy-based ink on acid-free recycled content paper, containing 10% POSTCONSUMER WASTE.

HOLT, RINEHART AND WINSTON

A Harcourt Classroom Education Company

Austin • New York • Orlando • Atlanta • San Francisco • Boston • Dallas • Toronto • London

Welcome!

Imagine that you have just entered a foreign land and culture. What better way to experience the unfamiliar territory than to find a knowledgeable guide? He or she could point out beautiful landscapes and historical landmarks while dazzling you with interesting tidbits about the region. Your guide could help you make the most of your visit and help make it a visit you'll remember.

Well you *have* just entered a foreign land! You've entered the land of *Holt Science & Technology: Life Science.* To help you make the most of your journey, use this booklet as your personal guide. Your guide will help you focus your attention on interesting images and important scientific facts. Your guide will also offer tips to help you understand the local language and ask you questions along the way to make sure you don't miss anything.

So sit back and get ready to fully experience *Holt Science & Technology*! Don't worry, this guide knows the ropes—all you have to do is follow along!

Art Credits:
All work, unless otherwise noted, by Holt, Rinehart and Winston.
Abbreviated as follows: (t) top; (l) left; (r) right; (c) center; (bkgd) background.
Front cover (owl), Kim Taylor/Bruce Coleman, Inc.; (forest), Carr Clifton; (jaguar), ©Gerry Ellis/GerryEllis.com; Page 31 (t), Carlyn Iverson

Printed in the United States of America

ISBN 0-03-055662-7   12 13 14 15   170   06 05 04 03

▪ CONTENTS ▪

Name _____ Date _____ Class_____

The World of Life Science

As you read Chapter 1, which begins on page 4 of your textbook, answer the following questions.

Imagine . . . (p. 4)

1. When students from Le Sueur, Minnesota, visited a wildlife refuge, they noticed something very strange. What did they notice?

_____

_____

What Do You Think? (p. 5)

Answer these questions in your ScienceLog now. Then later, you'll have a chance to revise your answers based on what you've learned.

Investigate! (p. 5)

2. What is the purpose of this activity?

_____

_____

_____

Section 1: Asking About Life (p. 6)

3. Suppose it is a slightly overcast afternoon and you decide to go fishing with a friend at a nearby stream. What is one example of a life-science question that might pop into your head along the way?

_____

_____

_____

4. Life science is the study of _____ things.

It All Starts with a Question (p. 6)

5. The existence of one-celled algae, giant redwood trees, and 40-ton whales illustrates the _____ of life.

6. How is the student shown on the left of the page doing life science?

_____

_____

Looking for Answers (p. 7)

Mark each of the following statements *True* or *False*.

7. _____ Anyone can be a life scientist.

8. _____ Life science investigations are done only in a laboratory.

9. _____ Life scientists study only how organisms function.

Why Ask Why? (p. 8)

10. Studying the human genome will help scientists learn about diseases such as cystic fibrosis, which are

_____ . (contracted or inherited)

11. What is the primary cause of most environmental problems?

_____

_____

_____

12. Why is Dale Miquelle concerned about trees being cut down?

_____

_____

_____

_____

Review (p. 9)

Now that you've finished Section 1, review what you learned by answering the Review questions in your ScienceLog.

Section 2: Thinking Like a Life Scientist (p. 10)

1. What are the first steps of the scientific method?

_____

_____

The Scientific Method (p. 10)

After you finish reading pages 10–17, answer the following questions, which are based on a fictional situation. Choose the step of the scientific method in Column B that best matches the example in Column A, and write the corresponding letter in the space provided.

Column A	Column B
____ **2.** Write an article describing what you learned about the ant population on school grounds.	**a.** Ask a question.
____ **3.** Last week there were no ants near the front door of our school. Now there is a large colony. Where did the colony come from?	**b.** Form a hypothesis.
____ **4.** I think someone released ants from their ant farm near the front door of our school.	**c.** Test the hypothesis.
____ **5.** There are a total of three ant colonies on the school grounds. Four of the 10 residents who live near the school also have ant colonies in their yard. The residents are neighbors; they live next door to one another on the same side of the street. None of the residents has ever owned an ant farm. None of the students surveyed had any information about where the ants came from.	**d.** Analyze the results.
	e. Draw conclusions.
____ **6.** Evidence seems to indicate that our rivals, the Hornets, placed the ant colony on our school grounds.	**f.** Communicate results.
____ **7.** I am examining the school grounds and surveying students and nearby residents for information about where the ants came from.	

8. After reading all of the steps in the scientific method described in questions 2–7 above, do you agree with the conclusion? Why or why not?

_____

_____

_____

_____

Scientific Knowledge Changes (p. 18)

Mark each of the following statements *True* or *False*.

9. _____ When a prediction is proven true, the related hypothesis is proven true.

10. _____ When scientists arrive at contradictory conclusions about the same experimental results, more research may be needed.

11. _____ New technology has proven that Neanderthals were our ancestors.

Review (p. 18)

Now that you've finished Section 2, review what you learned by answering the Review questions in your ScienceLog.

Section 3: Tools of Life Scientists (p. 19)

1. What do life scientists use tools for?

_____

_____

_____

Tools for Seeing (p. 19)

Answer the following questions after you finish reading Tools for Seeing on pages 19–21. Choose the term in Column B that best matches the phrase in Column A, and write the corresponding letter in the space provided.

Column A	Column B
____ **2.** bounces electrons off the surface of a specimen to produce a three-dimensional image	**a.** magnetic resonance imaging
____ **3.** passes electrons through a specimen to produce a flat image	**b.** computed tomography scan
____ **4.** made up of three main parts: a tube with lenses, a stage, and a light	**c.** scanning electron microscope
____ **5.** passes low-dosage X rays through the body at different angles	**d.** compound light microscope
____ **6.** uses short bursts of a magnetic field to produce images	**e.** transmission electron microscope

Computers (p. 21)

7. When was the first electronic computer built?

_____

8. Which of the following are ways in which life scientists use computers? (Circle all that apply.)

   a. to solve complex mathematical problems
   b. to share data and ideas
   c. to analyze information
   d. to store information
   e. to create graphs

Systems of Measurement (p. 22)

9. At one time, the English used three grains of barley arranged end

to end to represent _____ .

10. The units of the modern English system of measurement were

once based on the parts of the human body. True or False? (Circle one.)

11. Look at Figure 20 on page 23. Which unit of measurement is most practical for measuring an amoeba?

   a. nanometers (nm)   **c.** centimeters (cm)
   b. meters (m)   **d.** micrometers (μm)

12. What formula would you use to find out how much carpet is needed to cover the floor of your classroom?

_____

13. The units for area are called _____ units.

14. Before you can determine how many hippos will fit into a moving crate, you need two pieces of information. What are they?

_____

_____

_____

15. Which of the following is not a valid unit of measurement for volume?

   a. square micrometer   **c.** milliliter
   b. cubic centimeter   **d.** liter

16. Would you measure the mass of a hippopotamus in milligrams? If not, what unit would you use?

_____

_____

_____

_____

17. Look at Figure 25 on page 26. Water boils at 212 _____

or 100 _____ .

Safety Rules! (p. 27)

Match the following labels with the appropriate symbols.

_____ **18.** hand safety

_____ **19.** sharp object   **a.** ⬦

_____ **20.** clothing protection   **b.** ⬦

_____ **21.** chemical safety   **c.** ⬦

_____ **22.** eye protection   **d.** ⬦

_____ **23.** electrical safety   **e.** ⬦

_____ **24.** plant safety   **f.** ⬦

_____ **25.** heating safety   **g.** ⬦

_____ **26.** animal safety   **h.** ⬦

                                      i. ⬦

Review (p. 27)

Now that you've finished Section 3, review what you learned by answering the Review questions in your ScienceLog.

CHAPTER

2 DIRECTED READING WORKSHEET

It's Alive!! Or, Is It?

As you read Chapter 2, which begins on page 34 of your textbook, answer the following questions.

Imagine . . . (p. 34)

1. The creatures in the Movile Cave are different from most other life-forms on Earth because
   a. their energy supply comes from hydrogen sulfide.
   b. their energy supply comes from sunlight.
   c. they use energy to fuel their life processes.
   d. some of them eat their own young for energy.

2. According to the text, what will you study in this chapter?

   _____

   _____

What Do You Think? (p. 35)

Answer these questions in your ScienceLog now. Then later, you'll have a chance to revise your answers based on what you've learned.

Investigate! (p. 35)

3. What is going to be observed in this activity?

   _____

   _____

   _____

Section 1: Characteristics of Living Things (p. 36)

4. What might you have in common with a slime mold?

   _____

   _____

   _____

5. All organisms, including fish, trees, and mushrooms, share

   _____ characteristics.

CHAPTER 2

1 **All Living Things Have Cells** (p. 36)

In the space provided, write *AT* if the statement is always true,
ST if the statement is sometimes true, and *NT* if the statement is
never true.

6. _____ A cell has a membrane that acts as a barrier between its
contents and its environment.

7. _____ Complex organisms such as monkeys and humans are
made up of a few hundred cells.

8. _____ Living things have more than one cell.

9. _____ A cell is too small to be seen without a microscope.

10. _____ A cell performs all the basic functions of life.

11. _____ Cells perform specialized functions, such as transporting
signals and movement.

2 **All Living Things Sense and Respond to Change** (p. 37)

12. Organisms respond to changes in their environments called
stimuli. What are three examples of stimuli given in the text?

_____

_____

_____

13. The chemical reactions that happen inside your body can also

take place in any other type of environment. True or False?

(Circle one.)

14. When it is hot, your body sweats to maintain a temperature of

about 37°C. True or False? (Circle one.)

3 **All Living Things Reproduce** (p. 38)

15. Suppose the abalone reproduces by "broadcast spawning." The
female shoots eggs into the water, and the male shoots sperm
into the water. Is this sexual or asexual reproduction? Explain.

_____

_____

_____

_____

4 **All Living Things Have DNA** (p. 38)

16. Deoxyribonucleic acid provides instructions for making

molecules called _____ .

17. When they reproduce, organisms pass on copies of their

_____ to their offspring.

18. Offspring resemble their parents because of heredity.

True or False? (Circle one.)

5 **All Living Things Use Energy** (p. 38)

19. Which of the following statements are true about metabolism?
(Circle all that apply.)

a. It requires energy.
b. It is the sum of an organism's chemical activities.
c. It is directly involved in heredity.
d. It occurs only in multicellular organisms.
e. It involves the breakdown of food.

6 **All Living Things Grow and Develop** (p. 39)

20. Growth in humans takes place as their cells divide and produce
more cells. How do single-celled organisms grow?

_____

_____

21. Living things, such as the oak tree in Figure 7, may

_____ and _____

as they grow.

Review (p. 39)

Now that you've finished Section 1, review what you learned by
answering the Review questions in your ScienceLog.

Section 2: The Simple Bare Necessities of Life (p. 40)

1. You have the same basic needs as a tree. True or False?
(Circle one.)

2. What are the basic needs of a frog?

_____

_____

CHAPTER 2

Food (p. 40)

Choose the term in Column B that best matches the phrase in
Column A, and write the corresponding letter in the space provided.
Terms can be used more than once.

Column A	Column B
_____ **3.** eats other living organisms	**a.** producer
_____ **4.** grass	**b.** consumer
_____ **5.** breaks down nutrients in dead organisms	**c.** decomposer
_____ **6.** uses energy from the sun or the chemicals in the environment to make food	
_____ **7.** a salamander	
_____ **8.** the microorganisms in Movile Cave	

Water (p. 40)

9. The cells of cactuses, camels, and dragonflies are approximately

_____ percent water.

10. You get water from the foods you eat and the fluids you drink.
How many days could you survive without water?

_____

_____

Air (p. 41)

11. Respiration, which releases energy from food, requires

_____ . (carbon dioxide or oxygen)

12. Plants do not need oxygen to stay alive. True or False?
(Circle one.)

13. To make food during photosynthesis, green plants need all of the
following EXCEPT

    a. carbon dioxide.   **c.** water.

    b. sunlight.   **d.** oxygen.

A Place to Live (p. 41)

14. What do organisms need in the space where they live?

_____

_____

15. Look at Figure 10. What does the warbler's song mean to other warblers?

_____

_____

Review (p. 41)

Now that you've finished Section 2, review what you learned by answering the Review questions in your ScienceLog.

Section 3: The Chemistry of Life (p. 42)

1. Atoms are made up of molecules. True or False? (Circle one.)

2. What five compounds are in all cells?

_____

_____

Proteins (p. 42)

Choose the term in Column B that best matches the phrase in Column A, and write the corresponding letter in the space provided.

Column A	Column B
____ **3.** make up proteins	**a.** hemoglobin
____ **4.** proteins that speed up chemical reactions	**b.** water
____ **5.** protein found in red blood cells that attaches to oxygen	**c.** amino acids
____ **6.** more abundant in cells than protein	**d.** enzymes

Carbohydrates (p. 43)

7. Cells use carbohydrates, a group of compounds made of

_____ , to store energy and to use as a

source of _____ .

8. Look at the Brain Food in the right column of page 43. Your

_____ is determined by carbohydrates attached to proteins on your red blood cells.

9. Carbohydrates made of one sugar molecule are called

_____ carbohydrates. (simple or complex)

Chapter 2, continued

10. In terms of carbohydrates, what are you eating when you eat mashed potatoes?

_____

_____

_____

Lipids (p. 44)

Mark each of the following statements *True* or *False.*

11. _____ Lipids mix easily with water.

12. _____ Some lipids store energy for the cell.

13. _____ Usually, animals store lipids in the form of oil while plants store lipids in the form of fat.

14. _____ Special lipids, called phospholipids, form the membrane that surrounds cells.

15. _____ When phospholipid molecules come together in water, they form two layers.

Nucleic Acids (p. 45)

16. Why are nucleic acids called the blueprints of life?

_____

_____

_____

17. DNA, which contains information about how to make proteins, is a nucleic acid. True or False? (Circle one.)

The Cell's "Gasoline" (p. 45)

18. All cell activities that require _____ are fueled by a molecule called ATP.

19. Cells must transfer the energy in lipids to ATP before the cells can use the energy. True or False? (Circle one.)

Review (p. 45)

Now that you've finished Section 3, review what you learned by answering the Review questions in your ScienceLog.

CHAPTER

3 DIRECTED READING WORKSHEET

Light and Living Things

As you read Chapter 3, which begins on page 52 of your textbook, answer the following questions.

Strange but True! (p. 52)

1. The baby in the picture has jaundice. All of the following are true of jaundice EXCEPT
   a. it is caused by a buildup of bilirubin in the skin.
   b. it causes babies' skin to turn bluish.
   c. it is treated with blue light.
   d. if left untreated, it can cause brain damage.

2. What is a "bili blanket?"

   _____

   _____

   _____

   _____

What Do You Think? (p. 53)

Answer these questions in your ScienceLog now. Then later, you'll have a chance to revise your answers based on what you've learned.

Investigate! (p. 53)

3. What happens to light that passes through a spectroscope?

   _____

   _____

   _____

Section 1: The Electromagnetic Spectrum (p. 54)

4a. Bees can see something that you can't see. What is it?

   _____

   b. How are bees affected by the answer to (a)?

   _____

   _____

5. All electromagnetic waves are the same type. True or False?
   (Circle one.)

Waves Carry Energy (p. 54)

6. Earthquakes are caused by _____ waves.

7. The energy of a wave can cause matter to move. True or False?
   (Circle one.)

8. Although sound waves travel through the air, the air does not
   travel with the sound. What would happen every time you heard
   the phone ring if air did travel with sound?

   _____

   _____

   _____

9. Look at Figure 2. A leaf floating on the surface of a lake doesn't

   move toward the shore with the waves. True or False?
   (Circle one.)

Each of the following statements describes mechanical or electromagnetic waves. In the space provided, write *M* for a mechanical
wave and *E* for an electromagnetic wave.

10. _____   water waves, for example

11. _____   travel fastest through empty space

12. _____   can transfer energy without traveling through a medium

13. _____   radio waves, for example

14. _____   require a substance through which to travel

Electromagnetic Waves (p. 56)

15. In a vacuum, all electromagnetic waves travel at the speed of

    light. True or False? (Circle one.)

16. Light travels slower in glass than it does in space.

    True or False? (Circle one.)

17. An electromagnetic wave's _____ and

    _____ are used to classify it.

18. Usually waves that have _____ frequencies

    and _____ wavelengths carry the most
    energy.

19. Using the diagram of the electromagnetic spectrum on pages 56–57, arrange the following waves in order from shortest to longest wavelength: X rays, microwaves, gamma rays, visible light, radio waves.

_____

_____

20. Which one of the following colors of visible light carries the most energy?

   a. red   d. green
   b. orange   e. blue
   c. yellow   f. violet

21. Plants use visible light to make their own food. True or False? (Circle one.)

22. Why might you think of the name *Roy G. Biv* when you look at a rainbow?

_____

_____

_____

_____

_____

_____

23. Ultraviolet light makes up about _____ percent of the energy from the sun.

Mark each of the following statements *True* or *False*.

24. _____ Ultraviolet light carries less energy than visible light.

25. _____ Bacteria can be killed by ultraviolet light.

26. _____ Limited exposure to ultraviolet light helps your body make calcium.

27. _____ Too much ultraviolet light causes sunburn.

28. _____ Ultraviolet light is completely blocked by clouds.

Review (p. 58)
Now that you've finished Section 1, review what you learned by answering the Review questions in your ScienceLog.

Section 2: Reflection, Absorption, and Scattering (p. 59)

1. Why do a cat's eyes seem to glow in the dark?

_____

_____

_____

Reflection (p. 59)

2. Light waves are the only type of waves that reflect off objects.

True or False? (Circle one.)

3. How does reflection enable you to see objects?

_____

_____

_____

Use the text and Figures 6 and 7 on pages 59–60 to answer questions 4–8. Each of the following statements is false. Change the underlined words to make the statement true, and write the new word(s) in the space provided.

4. When light hits a mirror, its angle of incidence is <u>greater than</u> its angle of reflection.

_____

5. The <u>absorption</u> of a beam of light on a surface is called incidence.

_____

6. The angle between the reflected beam and the normal is called the angle of <u>incidence</u>.

_____

7. Light beams strike all points of a very <u>rough</u> surface at the same angle.

_____

8. When light beams are reflected at the same angle, it is called <u>diffuse</u> reflection.

_____

Chapter 3, continued

Absorption and Scattering (p. 60)

9. Why does a flashlight beam seem to weaken as it travels farther away from a flashlight?

_____

_____

_____

_____

_____

Read pages 60–61. Each of the following descriptions is true of either scattering or absorption. In the space provided, write *S* for scattering and *A* for absorption.

10. _____ the release of light energy by particles of matter that have absorbed extra energy

11. _____ causes light to go in all directions

12. _____ the transfer of energy carried by light waves to particles in matter

13. _____ affects light with short wavelengths more than light with long wavelengths

14. _____ allows you to see objects that are located outside the flashlight beam

15. Why is the sky blue?

_____

_____

_____

_____

Light and Color (p. 61)

16. When you see a lime under white light, it appears white.

True or False? (Circle one.)

17. In transmission, light passes through _____ .

18. In Figure 9, the glass feels warm because the light is transmitted

through the window. True or False? (Circle one.)

▲ CHAPTER 3
▲
▲

19. The _____ of a light wave determines the color of the light.

20. The color of an object is determined by the color of the light that reaches your eyes after being reflected off the object.

True or False? (Circle one.)

21. Use the terms you've learned in this chapter to explain why the strawberry in Figure 10 looks red.

_____

_____

_____

_____

22. A _____ object absorbs all the colors of

white light and a _____ object reflects all the colors of white light.

Mixing Colors of Light (p. 63)

23. What three colors of light can be combined to form all colors of light, including white light?

　a. yellow   **d.** blue
　b. red   **e.** cyan
　c. magenta   **f.** green

24. _____ , a secondary color of light, is

formed when red and green, two _____ colors of light, are added together.

Mixing Colors of Pigment (p. 64)

25. Pigments, such as chlorophyll, give objects their

_____ .

26. What three colors of pigment can be combined to produce any color?

　a. yellow   **d.** blue
　b. red   **e.** cyan
　c. magenta   **f.** green

Review (p. 64)

Now that you've finished Section 2, review what you learned by answering the Review questions in your ScienceLog.

Section 3: Refraction (p. 65)

Place the following sentences in the appropriate order to show the steps that light takes to make an object visible to you. Write the appropriate number in the corresponding space.

1. _____ Light enters your eye through your pupil.

2. _____ Light forms an image on your retina.

3. _____ Light passes through your cornea and lens.

4. _____ Light reflects off an object.

Rays Show the Path of Light Waves (p. 65)

5. A ray is an arrow that shows the path and

_____ of a light wave.

6. Since light waves travel in straight lines, they cannot change

direction. True or False? (Circle one.)

Refraction (p. 66)

7. Light travels at different speeds through different media.

True or False? (Circle one.)

8. Why is the beam of light in Figure 14 bent?

_____

_____

_____

_____

9. Light waves with _____ wavelengths are

bent less than light waves with _____
wavelengths.

10. White light can be separated into different colors during refraction because the different colors that make up white light have

different wavelengths. True or False? (Circle one.)

11. What causes a rainbow?

_____

_____

_____

_____

CHAPTER 3

Lenses Refract Light (p. 67)

12. Which of the following are characteristics of lenses?
(Circle all that apply.)

a. They are flat.   **c.** They are reflective.
b. They are curved.   **d.** They are transparent.

After you finish reading page 67, choose the type of lens in Column B that matches the description in Column A, and write the corresponding letter in the space provided. Lenses can be used more than once.

Column A	Column B
____ **13.** helps people who are nearsighted	**a.** convex lens
____ **14.** focuses light inside your eye	**b.** concave lens
____ **15.** thinner at the edges than at the middle	
____ **16.** thicker at the edges than at the middle	
____ **17.** refracts light toward its center	

Optical Instruments (p. 68)

18. Optical instruments use arrangements of

_____ and _____
to help people make observations.

Using Figure 19 as a reference, mark the following statements *True* or *False*.

19. _____ The longer the shutter of a camera is open, the more light that enters the camera.

20. _____ More light enters the camera when the aperture is small than when the aperture is large.

21. _____ The lens of a camera is a concave lens.

22. There are two kinds of telescopes. _____ telescopes use mirrors to collect light, and

_____ telescopes use lenses to collect light.

23. What is the difference between microscopes and telescopes?

a. Microscopes have an objective lens.
b. Microscopes have an eyepiece lens.
c. Microscopes produce a magnified image.
d. Microscopes are used to look at tiny, nearby objects.

Review (p. 69)

Now that you've finished Section 3, review what you learned by answering the Review questions in your ScienceLog.

CHAPTER

4 ■ DIRECTED READING WORKSHEET

Cells: The Basic Units of Life

As you read Chapter 4, which begins on page 78 of your textbook, answer the following questions.

What if . . .? (p. 78)

1. Where does Dr. Margulis think the energy-producing structures in cells came from?

_____

_____

_____

_____

_____

_____

2. What will you study in this chapter?

_____

_____

_____

What Do You Think? (p. 79)

Answer these questions in your ScienceLog now. Then later, you'll have a chance to revise your answers based on what you've learned.

Investigate! (p. 79)

3. What type of cells are used in this activity?

    a. plant cells   **c.** dog cells
    b. frog cells   **d.** human cells

Section 1: Organization of Life (p. 80)

4. All of the items necessary for _____ are contained in a single cell.

CHAPTER 4

▲
▲▲
▲

Cells: Starting Out Small (p. 80)

Mark each of the following statements *True* or *False*.

5. _____ All cells are too small to be seen without a microscope.

6. _____ You began as a single cell.

7. _____ All your cells look and act the same.

8. Look at Figure 2. How many cells do you have in your body?

_____

_____

Tissues: Cells Working in Teams (p. 81)

9. Cells that have similar functions group together to form

_____ .

10. What are three examples of cells that make up tissues pictured in the text?

_____

Organs: Teams Working Together (p. 81)

11. Organs are made up of groups of _____ .

12. Look at Figure 4. Your _____ is the largest and most visible organ in your body.

Organ Systems: A Great Combination (p. 82)

13. What is an organ system?

_____

_____

_____

14. What would happen if your digestive system stopped working?

_____

_____

_____

_____ **Chapter 4, continued** _____

Organisms: Independent Living (p. 83)

15. Some organisms are made of one cell. True or False? (Circle one.)

16. Are the cells of your body considered organisms? Why or why not?

_____

_____

_____

17. You are an example of a unicellular organism. True or False? (Circle one.)

The Big Picture (p. 83)

Choose the term in Column B that best matches the example or definition in Column A, and write the corresponding letter in the space provided. Terms may be used more than once.

Column A	Column B
_____ **18.** an ocean	**a.** organism
_____ **19.** the people, dogs, and cats in a town	**b.** population
_____ **20.** a group of organisms of the same kind that live in the same area	**c.** community
_____ **21.** all the ladybird beetles in the forest	**d.** ecosystem
_____ **22.** the soil, rocks, trees, ladybird beetles, and other organisms in a forest	
_____ **23.** a ladybird beetle	
_____ **24.** groups of organisms living in the same area and the nonliving things that affect them	
_____ **25.** a dog	
_____ **26.** two or more different groups of organisms living in the same area	
_____ **27.** the oak trees, flowers, lizards, and other organisms in a forest	

Review (p. 84)

Now that you've finished Section 1, review what you learned by answering the Review questions in your ScienceLog.

▲▲ CHAPTER 4

Section 2: The Discovery of Cells (p. 85)

1. Why were cells discovered by accident?

_____

_____

Seeing the First Cells (p. 85)

2. What did Robert Hooke see when he looked at a thin slice of cork with his compound microscope?

_____

_____

3. *Cell* means _____ in Latin.

4. Did Hooke think that cells were found in all organisms? Explain.

_____

_____

_____

_____

Seeing Cells in Other Life-Forms (p. 86)

5. Anton van Leeuwenhoek did NOT

   a. see bacteria.
   b. discover that frog and human blood cells are the same shape.
   c. discover that yeast are unicellular organisms.
   d. see small organisms in pond scum.

The Cell Theory (p. 86)

6. When did scientists realize that all organisms contain cells?

_____

_____

_____

7. The basic unit of _____ in all living things is the cell.

8. Rudolf Virchow realized that all cells come from

_____ cells.

Chapter 4, continued

Cell Similarities (p. 87)

Choose the cell feature in Column B that best matches the phrase in Column A, and write the corresponding letter in the space provided.

Column A	Column B
____ **9.** barrier between the inside of a cell and its environment	**a.** cytoplasm
____ **10.** structures a cell uses to live, grow, and reproduce	**b.** cell membrane
____ **11.** the fluid in a cell and almost everything in the fluid	**c.** DNA
____ **12.** controls all activities of a cell and contains the information needed for a cell to make new cells	**d.** organelles

Giant Amoeba Eats New York City (p. 88)

13. Could an amoeba become large enough to eat New York City? Why or why not?

_____

_____

_____

_____

_____

_____

14. In addition to being able to grow larger, what is another benefit of being multicellular?

_____

_____

_____

_____

_____

CHAPTER 4

Chapter 4, continued

Two Types of Cells (p. 90)

Answer the following questions after reading pages 90–91.
Each of the following statements is false. Change the underlined
word to make the statement true. Write the new word in the space
provided.

15. Eukaryotic cells have <u>circular</u> DNA.

_____

16. Prokaryotic cells contain <u>membrane-covered organelles</u> that
make proteins.

_____

17. <u>Cell walls</u> surround all eukaryotic cells.

_____

18. A eukaryotic cell has DNA inside the <u>ribosome</u>.

_____

19. Prokaryotic cells are also called <u>algae</u>.

_____

Review (p. 91)

Now that you've finished Section 2, review what you learned by
answering the Review questions in your ScienceLog.

Section 3: Eukaryotic Cells: The Inside Story (p. 92)

1. What two things helped scientists see more cell detail?

_____

_____

_____

Holding It All Together (p. 92)

2. Which of the following is NOT a function of the cell membrane?

   a. It brings nutrients inside the cell and lets out waste products.
   b. It prevents the cell wall from tearing.
   c. It keeps the cytoplasm inside the cell.
   d. It interacts with things outside the cell.

3. Considering that trees don't have bones, how do they stand up
straight?

_____

_____

The Cell's Library (p. 93)

4. In a eukaryotic cell, the largest organelle is the

_____ .

5. The dark spot inside the nucleus is the

_____ .

6. Why do you think the nucleus is called the cell's library?

_____

_____

_____

Protein Factories (p. 94)

7. Would cells die if they didn't have ribosomes? Explain.

_____

_____

The Cell's Delivery System (p. 94)

8. What are the functions of the endoplasmic reticulum?
(Circle all that apply.)

   a. It stores DNA.
   b. It makes lipids.
   c. It moves substances to different places in the cell.
   d. It breaks down harmful chemicals.

9. _____ cause the surface of some ER to look rough.

The Cell's Power Plants (p. 95)

10. The _____ from broken-down food molecules is transferred to a special molecule called ATP.

11. Mitochondria need _____ to make ATP.

12. A chloroplast is an energy-converting organelle found in

_____ and _____ .

13. According to the endosymbiotic theory, mitochondria and chloroplasts originated as bacteria. True or False? (Circle one.)

The Cell's Packaging Center (p. 96)

14. The Golgi complex processes, packages, and transports materials

sent to it from the _____ .

CHAPTER 4

The Cell's Storage Centers (p. 97)

15. Where do vesicles come from?

_____

_____

_____

_____

16. Why does wilted lettuce become crispy when it is soaked in water?

_____

_____

_____

Packages of Destruction (p. 98)

17. Lysosomes do NOT

    a. contain enzymes.   **c.** destroy damaged organelles.

    b. store liquids in the cell.   **d.** protect the cell from invaders.

18. Why don't humans have webbed fingers?

_____

_____

_____

Plant or Animal? (p. 99)

19. If you look at a cell through a microscope, how can you tell whether it is a plant cell or an animal cell?

_____

_____

_____

Review (p. 99)

Now that you've finished Section 3, review what you learned by answering the Review questions in your ScienceLog.

DIRECTED READING WORKSHEET

The Cell in Action

As you read Chapter 5, which begins on page 106 of your textbook, answer the following questions.

What If . . . ? (p. 106)

1. Scientists have found an enzyme that acts like a cellular fountain of youth. What can this enzyme do?

_____

_____

_____

_____

_____

What Do You Think? (p. 107)

Answer these questions in your ScienceLog now. Then later, you'll have a chance to revise your answers based on what you've learned.

Investigate! (p. 107)

2. Yeast are fungi that eat _____ and produce

   the gas _____ .

Section 1: Exchange with the Environment (p. 108)

3. How is a cell like a factory?

_____

_____

_____

What Is Diffusion? (p. 108)

4. Look at Figure 1. Why does the line between the dye and the gelatin blur?

_____

_____

_____

_____

5. Particles naturally travel from areas of

_____ concentration to areas of

_____ concentration.

6. Osmosis is the _____ of

_____ through the cell membrane.

7. The particles of food coloring in Figure 2 are too large to move

through the barrier. True or False? (Circle one.)

8. How do water, salts, and sugars keep a blood cell from swelling?

_____

_____

_____

_____

_____

9. How does a wilted plant "drink" water?

_____

_____

_____

Moving Small Particles (p. 110)

10. Which of the following particles use special protein "doorways"
to pass through the cell membrane? (Circle all that apply.)

    a. amino acids   **c.** water

    b. oxygen   **d.** sugar

After you finish reading page 110, indicate whether each of the
following statements describes active or passive transport by writing
A for active or *P* for passive in the space provided.

11. _____ uses energy from the molecule ATP

12. _____ diffusion of particles through proteins

13. _____ the way sugar enters a cell if there is more sugar outside
the cell than inside the cell

14. _____ the movement of particles from an area of low
concentration to an area of high concentration

15. _____ no energy used by the cell

Moving Large Particles (p. 111)

Use the figures below to answer the following questions.

Figure A   Figure B   Figure C

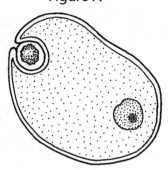 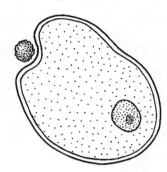 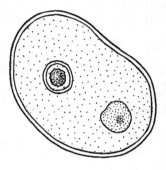

16. In which order would the figures demonstrate exocytosis?

_____

17. In which order would the figures demonstrate endocytosis?

_____

Review (p. 111)

Now that you've finished Section 1, review what you learned by answering the Review questions in your ScienceLog.

Section 2: Cell Energy (p. 112)

1. What is your body telling you when you feel hungry?

_____

_____

From Sun to Cell (p. 112)

2. Does your body need plants for energy? Why or why not?

_____

_____

_____

_____

CHAPTER 5

3. Which of the following statements describe chlorophyll? (Circle all that apply.)

    a. It is a green pigment.
    b. It is found in mitochondria.
    c. It absorbs light energy.
    d. It is found in plant cells.

4. Plant cells can store some energy in the form of lipids or

carbohydrates. True or False? (Circle one.)

5. Which of the following are products of photosynthesis? (Circle all that apply.)

    a. glucose   **d.** carbon dioxide
    b. light energy   **e.** water
    c. oxygen   **f.** ATP

Getting Energy from Food (p. 113)

6. How can your body get energy from a banana?

_____

_____

_____

_____

7. Cellular respiration does not use oxygen. True or False? (Circle one.)

8. How does breathing help your cells perform cellular respiration?

_____

_____

_____

_____

9. Which of the following are NOT released during cellular respiration? (Circle all that apply.)

    a. carbon dioxide   **d.** oxygen
    b. water   **e.** glucose
    c. chlorophyll   **f.** energy

10. ATP is a type of molecule that supplies energy to cells.

True or False? (Circle one.)

Chapter 5, continued

11. What does your body do with the heat released during cellular respiration?

_____

_____

_____

12. Cellular respiration occurs only in animal cells. True or False? (Circle one.)

13. Cellular respiration in animals takes place in the

_____ inside the cell.

Use the diagram on page 114 to answer questions 14–19. Choose the term in Column B that best matches the description in Column A, and write the corresponding letter in the space provided.

Column A	Column B
_____ **14.** Glucose is made inside this structure.	**a.** mitochondrion
_____ **15.** Oxygen is released during this process.	**b.** ATP
_____ **16.** This is needed along with light and CO_2 for photosynthesis.	**c.** cellular respiration
_____ **17.** This molecule stores energy so cells can use it.	**d.** water
_____ **18.** This structure produces ATP.	**e.** chloroplast
_____ **19.** Energy is released during this process.	**f.** photosynthesis

20. Why do you get sore muscles when you exercise a lot or after strenuous activities?

_____

_____

_____

_____

_____

21. How did fermentation help the bread in Figure 11 rise?

_____

_____

_____

_____

_____

Review (p. 115)

Now that you've finished Section 2, review what you learned by answering the Review questions in your ScienceLog.

Section 3: The Cell Cycle (p. 116)

1. Why is it important for your body to produce millions of new cells by the time you finish reading this sentence?

_____

_____

_____

The Life of a Cell (p. 116)

2. The life cycle of a cell, known as the _____ ,

begins when the cell is _____ and ends

when the cell _____ and forms new cells.

3. How does each new cell get its tools for survival?

_____

_____

_____

Mark each of the following statements *True* or *False*.

4. _____ Bacteria have a single membrane-covered organelle.

5. _____ Prokaryotic cells divide by binary fission.

6. _____ Eukaryotic cells have more DNA than prokaryotic cells.

7. _____ The chromosomes of eukaryotic cells contain only DNA.

Chapter 5, continued

8. A potato cell has more chromosomes than a human cell.

True or False? (Circle one.)

9. Look at the chromosomes in Figure 13. Each of your body cells contains

  a. 23 chromosomes.
  b. 46 pairs of homologous chromosomes.
  c. 23 pairs of homologous chromosomes.
  d. 48 chromosomes.

10. What's so special about pairs of homologous chromosomes?

_____

_____

11. In the beginning of the eukaryotic cell cycle, the cell grows and

duplicates its _____ and

_____ .

12. Where are chromatids held together?

_____

_____

13. Mitosis is all of the following EXCEPT

  a. the process of chromosome separation.
  b. part of the second stage of the eukaryotic cell cycle.
  c. the process during which the cell divides.
  d. the process by which each new cell gets a copy of each chromosome.

14. The cell _____ in the third stage of the eukaryotic cell cycle.

15. How are the two new cells produced by mitosis related to the original cell?

_____

_____

Mitosis and the Cell Cycle (p. 118)

16. Before mitosis begins, what two types of paired cell structures are copied?

_____

_____

CHAPTER 5

Use the diagrams on pages 118 and 119 to answer questions 17–20.
Put the phases of mitosis in order by labeling them as Phase 1,
Phase 2, Phase 3, or Phase 4.

17. _____ The fibers attached to the centrioles pull the
chromatids to opposite sides of the cell.

18. _____ The chromosomes line up along the equator of
the cell.

19. _____ The nuclear membrane forms around the two sets
of chromosomes, and the chromosomes unwind.
The fibers disappear.

20. _____ The two pairs of centrioles move to opposite sides
of the cell, and fibers form between them. The
fibers attach to the centromeres.

21. What does pinching have to do with the cell splitting in two?

_____

_____

_____

_____

Place the following structures in the order in which they form in
eukaryotic cells with cell walls during cytokinesis. Write the appropriate number in the space provided.

22. _____ cell wall

23. _____ cell plate

24. _____ cell membrane

Review (p. 119)

Now that you've finished Section 3, review what you learned by
answering the Review questions in your ScienceLog.

CHAPTER

6 | DIRECTED READING WORKSHEET

Heredity

As you read Chapter 6, which begins on page 128 of your textbook, answer the following questions.

Would You Believe . . . ? (p. 128)

1. What happened when a Chinese fisherman took two gold-tinged carp home?

   a. The fish fought, and the more brightly colored fish won.
   b. The fish reproduced, and the offspring were more brightly colored than the parents.
   c. The fish reproduced, and the offspring had a very drab color.
   d. The fish could not survive in captivity.

2. Early goldfish breeders were using the principles of

   _____ to create new types of goldfish.

What Do You Think? (p. 129)

Answer these questions in your ScienceLog now. Then later, you'll have a chance to revise your answers based on what you've learned.

Investigate! (p. 129)

3. The purpose of this activity is to see how different

   _____ can be combined to create something unique.

Section 1: Mendel and His Peas (p. 130)

4. You don't look exactly like anyone else, unless you are an identical twin. Why do you think that is true?

   _____

   _____

   _____

Why Don't You Look Like a Rhinoceros? (p. 130)

5. How does heredity explain why you don't look like a rhinoceros?

   _____

   _____

   _____

Who Was Gregor Mendel? (p. 130)

6. In the garden of a monastery, Gregor Mendel studied how traits

are passed from _____ to

_____ .

Unraveling the Mystery (p. 131)

7. Mendel noticed that

    a. all of the parents' traits can be seen in their offspring.

    b. only plants have traits that don't appear in some generations.

    c. sometimes a trait will not appear in a generation.

    d. all traits appear in every generation.

8. What is a "self-pollinating" plant?

_____

_____

_____

_____

Peas Be My Podner (p. 132)

Mark each of the following statements *True* or *False*.

9. _____ Mendel chose to study several traits at one time to get as much information as possible.

10. _____ In Figure 4, wrinkled and round are the two traits shown for the characteristic of seed shape.

11. _____ If it self-pollinates, a tall true-breeding plant can produce short offspring.

12. _____ In cross-pollination, a plant's anthers are removed and it is fertilized with pollen from another plant.

Mendel's First Experiment (p. 133)

13. Look at Figure 6. What happened when Mendel crossed plants that had round seeds with plants that had wrinkled seeds?

_____

_____

14. For each characteristic, Mendel called the trait that always

appeared _____ and the trait that seemed

to disappear _____ .

Mendel's Second Experiment (p. 133)

15. When the first generation of plants was allowed to self-pollinate, as shown in Figure 6,

    a. all of the offspring had the recessive trait.

    b. some of the offspring had the recessive trait.

    c. all of the offspring had the dominant trait.

    d. the first-generation plants could not produce offspring.

A Different Point of View (p. 134)

16. Mendel counted the number of plants with each trait in the

    _____ generation.

17. Take a minute to read the Math Break on page 134. In the table of Mendel's results, the dominant-to-recessive ratio for each trait is

    a. about 1 : 3.   **c.** about 1 : 2.

    b. about 3 : 1.   **d.** about 2 : 1.

A Brilliant Idea (p. 135)

Choose the term in Column B that best matches the phrase in Column A, and write the corresponding letter in the space provided.

Column A	Column B
_____ **18.** used to visualize the combinations of alleles from the parents	**a.** genes
_____ **19.** the inherited combination of alleles	**b.** Punnett squares
_____ **20.** the organism's inherited appearance	**c.** genotype
_____ **21.** sets of instructions for inherited characteristics	**d.** phenotype

22. Look at Figure 8 on page 136. What combinations of alleles will result in plants with purple flowers?

    _____

    _____

What Are the Chances? (p. 136)

23. Offspring are more likely to inherit either of their alleles for each trait from the mother. True or False? (Circle one.)

24. The probability that you would toss two heads in a row with a coin is _____ percent.

25. Were Mendel's ideas immediately accepted by the scientific community when he published his results? Explain.

_____

_____

_____

26. Look at the Chemistry Connection on page 137.

_____ seeds do not convert sugar into

starch, so they are sweeter than _____
seeds.

Review (p. 137)

Now that you've finished Section 1, review what you learned by answering the Review questions in your ScienceLog.

Section 2: Meiosis (p. 138)

1. Understanding _____ was the first step in finding out where genes are located and how they pass information from one cell to another.

Two Kinds of Reproduction (p. 138)

Read "Two Kinds of Reproduction" on pages 138–139. Then mark each of the following statements *True* or *False*.

2. _____ Only one parent cell is needed for asexual reproduction.

3. _____ Most single-celled organisms reproduce through sexual reproduction.

4. _____ A human egg cell contains only half the chromosomes found inside a human body cell.

5. _____ During sexual reproduction, each parent donates one-half of a homologous pair of chromosomes to the offspring.

6. _____ When sex cells are made, the chromosomes are copied twice and the nucleus divides once.

Meanwhile, Back at the Lab (p. 139)

7. What was Walter Sutton's important proposal?

_____

_____

8. Take a moment to read "Mitosis Revisited" on page 139. Mitosis results in _____ exact copies of the original cell.

Meiosis in Eight Easy Steps (p. 140)

Answer the following questions after you finish reading pages 140 and 141. Place the following steps of meiosis in order by writing the appropriate number in the space provided.

9. _____ Paired homologous chromosomes line up at the cell's equator.

10. _____ Chromatids pull apart and move to opposite ends of each cell, and the cells divide.

11. _____ Four new cells are formed from one original cell.

12. _____ The cell divides, but the paired chromatids are still joined.

13. _____ Chromosomes separate from their homologous partners.

14. _____ Chromosomes thicken and shorten. The nuclear membrane disappears.

15. _____ Chromosomes line up at the equator.

16. _____ Each cell contains one member of each homologous chromosome pair.

Meiosis and Mendel (p. 142)

Use Figure 10 to answer the following questions.

17. What type of allele is in all of the sperm nuclei?

_____

_____

18. What type of allele is in all of the egg nuclei?

_____

_____

19. The first-generation plant in Figure 10 will have wrinkled seeds.
True or False? (Circle one.)

20. What genotype is the result of the fertilization of any egg by any sperm in Figure 10?

    a. *RR*   **b.** *Rr*   **c.** *rr*

Male or Female? (p. 143)

21. Human males have 23 matched pairs of chromosomes.

True or False? (Circle one.)

22. Are the chromosomes in Figure 11 from a male or a female? Explain.

_____

_____

_____

_____

23. How are female chromosomes different from male chromosomes?

_____

_____

_____

24. Look at Figure 12. If an egg is fertilized by a sperm containing an

X chromosome, the offspring will be a _____,
but if the sperm contains a Y chromosome, the offspring will be a

_____ .

Review (p. 143)

Now that you've finished Section 2, review what you learned by answering the Review questions in your ScienceLog.

CHAPTER
7 DIRECTED READING WORKSHEET

Genes and Gene Technology

As you read Chapter 7, which begins on page 150 of your textbook, answer the following questions.

What If . . . ? (p. 150)

1. How could DNA be helpful in a police investigation?

_____

_____

_____

What Do You Think? (p. 151)

Answer these questions in your ScienceLog now. Then later, you'll have a chance to revise your answers based on what you've learned.

Investigate! (p. 151)

2. What are the three most common fingerprint patterns among humans?

_____

_____

_____

Section 1: What Do Genes Look Like? (p. 152)

3. Where are the chromosomes found in most cells?

    a. the nucleus   **c.** the DNA

    b. the genes   **d.** the ribosomes

4. _____ and _____

    make up chromosomes.

The Pieces of the Puzzle (p. 152)

5. What two functions must the gene material be able to carry out?

_____

_____

_____

_____

_____

6. Scientists thought that proteins carried the hereditary information because

    a. proteins were simple molecules.
    b. proteins were complex molecules.
    c. DNA did not exist.
    d. DNA was a complex molecule.

7. Which of the following make up a nucleotide? (Circle all that apply.)

    a. a sugar   **c.** a phosphate
    b. a protein   **d.** a base

8. Except for the type of _____ present, all DNA nucleotides are identical.

9. Look at Figure 1. How do you think the nucleotides fit together in pairs?

_____

_____

_____

10. What did Chargaff discover about the bases of DNA nucleotides?

_____

_____

_____

_____

A Picture of DNA (p. 153)

11. Rosalind Franklin created images of DNA molecules that suggested DNA is _____ -shaped.

Eureka! (p. 153)

12. When Francis Crick said, "We have discovered the secret of life!" what was he talking about?

_____

_____

_____

_____

Chapter 7, continued

After you finish reading pages 152–153 in your text, answer questions 13–17. Choose the term in Column B that best matches the description in Column A, and write the corresponding letter in the space provided.

Column A	Column B
____ **13.** The amount of this base is equal to the amount of adenine in DNA.	**a.** cytosine
____ **14.** This is the shape of a DNA molecule.	**b.** thymine
____ **15.** The amount of this base is equal to the amount of guanine in DNA.	**c.** nucleotides
____ **16.** DNA is the major part of these structures.	**d.** double helix
____ **17.** These are the subunits of DNA.	**e.** chromosomes

DNA Structure (p. 154)

18. What part of the twisted ladder, or double helix, of DNA is made up of the nucleotide bases?

_____

_____

_____

19. Look at Figure 6. Does anything happen if the bases in the DNA molecule do not pair up correctly? Explain.

_____

_____

_____

Making Copies of DNA (p. 155)

20. After the DNA molecule splits down the middle, what happens so that two identical molecules of DNA are formed?

_____

_____

_____

CHAPTER 7

From Trait to Gene (p. 156)

Use pages 156–157 to answer the following questions.

Each of the following statements is false. Change the underlined word to make the statement true. Write the new word in the space provided.

21. Each gene is made up of a string of <u>proteins</u>.

_____

22. The cell gets information about how to make each trait from the <u>number</u> of the bases.

_____

23. Each human skin cell contains <u>64</u> chromosomes.

_____

24. Each <u>nucleotide</u> is made of protein and DNA.

_____

More News About Traits (p. 158)

25. There are no exceptions to Mendel's principles of how genes are

passed on from one generation to the next. True or False? (Circle one.)

26. Figure 8 shows a cross between a white snapdragon and a red snapdragon. Why are all the snapdragon offspring pink instead of white or red?

_____

_____

_____

27. Look at the picture of the tiger on page 158. What is the connection between the color of the white tiger's fur and the color of its eyes?

_____

_____

_____

_____

28. Look at the figure at the bottom of page 159. Why are there so many different shades of eye color?

_____

_____

_____

_____

_____

29. Genes are the only influences on your development.

True or False? (Circle one.)

Review (p. 159)

Now that you've finished Section 1, review what you learned by answering the Review questions in your ScienceLog.

Section 2: How DNA Works (p. 160)

1. The order of the bases in DNA forms a

_____ that tells the cell what to do.

Genes and Proteins (p. 160)

2. A group of three bases makes up the code for an amino

acid. True or False? (Circle one.)

3. The order of bases has no bearing on the order of amino acids in

a protein. True or False? (Circle one.)

4. What do proteins have to do with what you look like?

_____

_____

_____

_____

_____

5. There are about _____ genes in human

cells and about _____ different kinds of proteins in the human body.

The Making of a Protein (p. 161)

Place the following steps of protein formation in order by writing the appropriate number in the space provided.

6. _____ The genetic information from the section of DNA is taken to the cytoplasm.

7. _____ Transfer molecules bring amino acids from the cytoplasm to the ribosome.

8. _____ A section of the DNA strand containing a gene is copied.

9. _____ The copy of the DNA is fed through the ribosome.

10. _____ The amino acids join together in a long chain.

11. _____ The amino acids are dropped off at the ribosome.

Changes in Genes (p. 162)

12. Mutations are mistakes that occur in DNA. In what three ways do mutations happen?

_____

_____

_____

_____

13. Which of the following can happen if repair enzymes do not find and repair mistakes in the DNA? (Circle all that apply.)

a. There can be an improvement.

b. There can be a harmful change.

c. There can be no change at all.

14. List three examples of mutagens given in the text.

_____

_____

_____

_____

An Example of a Substitution (p. 163)

15. Substituting the _____ valine for glutamic acid in a blood protein causes sickle cell anemia.

16. Sickled red blood cells are not as good at carrying

_____ as normal red blood cells.

Genetic Counseling (p. 164)

17. To inherit a recessive hereditary disorder, a child must inherit a defective gene from

    a. one parent.   **c.** the mother.

    b. both parents.   **d.** the father.

18. What do genetic counselors use a pedigree for?

_____

_____

_____

_____

Review (p. 164)

Now that you've finished Section 2, review what you learned by answering the Review questions in your ScienceLog.

Section 3: Applied Genetics (p. 165)

1. Humans have used selective breeding for thousands of years. Use the text to list two examples of plants or animals that have been selectively bred.

_____

_____

_____

_____

_____

_____

Designer Genes (p. 165)

2. Look at Figure 15. Cloning is a form of genetic engineering.

True or False? (Circle one.)

3. Why does the tobacco plant shown in Figure 15 glow?

_____

_____

_____

_____

_____

_____

Living Factories (p. 166)

4. Recombinant DNA is the DNA that results when

_____ from one organism are put into another organism.

5. What happens when scientists put a normal human insulin gene in the DNA of a bacterium?

_____

_____

_____

_____

DNA Fingerprints (p. 166)

6. The DNA fragments shown in Figure 17 have been separated from each other based on their size. True or False? (Circle one.)

7. Only _____ can have the same DNA fingerprint.

The Big Picture (p. 167)

8. What is the goal of the Human Genome Project?

_____

_____

_____

Review (p. 167)

Now that you've finished Section 3, review what you learned by answering the Review questions in your ScienceLog.

CHAPTER

8 ⬛ **DIRECTED READING WORKSHEET**

The Evolution of Living Things

As you read Chapter 8, which begins on page 174 of your textbook, answer the following questions.

What If . . .? (p. 174)

1. Scientists think *Diatryma* probably became extinct because

    a. the population was weakened by disease.

    b. it was forced out of existence by large mammals.

    c. it was the favorite prey of dinosaurs.

    d. it was too large to survive.

What Do You Think? (p. 175)

Answer these questions in your ScienceLog now. Then later, you'll have a chance to revise your answers based on what you've learned.

Investigate! (p. 175)

2. The two types of fossils being modeled in this activity are a

_____ and a _____ .

Section 1: Change Over Time (p. 176)

3. Look at Figures 1–3 on this page. How does being bright red help the strawberry dart-poison frog survive?

_____

_____

_____

_____

_____

Differences Among Organisms (p. 176)

4. Can strawberry dart-poison frogs mate with red-eyed tree frogs to produce offspring? Why or why not?

_____

_____

_____

▲▲
▲
▲

CHAPTER 8

Chapter 8, continued

Read page 177 and look at Figure 4. Then, mark each of the following statements *True* or *False*.

5. _____ Scientists believe that all living things, including daisies, crocodiles, and humans, share a common ancestor.

6. _____ A great number of species have died out since life first appeared on Earth.

7. _____ The first mammals appeared on Earth at about the same time as the first terrestrial plants.

Evidence of Evolution: The Fossil Record (p. 178)

8. What is one way fossils are formed?

_____

_____

_____

_____

9. Fossils found in the upper layers of the Earth's crust are

_____ than fossils found in the lower layers. (newer or older)

10. There are gaps in the fossil record because
   a. the conditions needed for fossils to form are rare.
   b. very few different organisms have lived on Earth.
   c. many fossils have been destroyed.
   d. not many people are looking for fossils.

Answer question 11 after reading about vestigial structures on page 179.

11. Which of the following are reasons that scientists think whales evolved from doglike land dwellers? (Circle all that apply.)
   a. Whales are mammals.
   b. Whales have vestigial hind-limb bones.
   c. Whales bark like dogs.
   d. There is fossil evidence to support evolution from doglike land dwellers.
   e. Whales are shaped like fish.

Name _____ Date _____ Class _____

Chapter 8, continued

Case Study: Evolution of the Whale (p. 180)

Complete this section after you finish reading pages 180 and 181. Choose the whale ancestor in Column B that matches the description in Column A, and write the corresponding letter in the space provided. Each answer can be used more than once.

Column A	Column B
___ **12.** could walk like a crocodile	**a.** *Mesonychid*
___ **13.** existed about 40 million years ago	**b.** *Ambulocetus*
___ **14.** kicked its legs like an otter does to swim	**c.** *Rodhocetus*
___ **15.** lived in coastal waters	**d.** *Prozeuglodon*
___ **16.** returned to the ocean about 55 million years ago	
___ **17.** was adapted for life at sea	
___ **18.** land-dwelling mammal	
___ **19.** spent most of its life in the water	

Evidence of Evolution: Comparing Organisms (p. 182)

20. Look at Figure 9. What similarities do you see among the bones of a human arm, the front leg of a cat, a dolphin flipper, and a bat wing?

_____

_____

_____

_____

21. All living organisms have the same type of

_____ .

22. All _____ look very similar when they are in the embryonic stage. (living things or vertebrates)

Review (p. 183)

Now that you've finished Section 1, review what you learned by answering the Review questions in your ScienceLog.

Copyright © by Holt, Rinehart and Winston. All rights reserved.

CHAPTER 8

DIRECTED READING WORKSHEETS **53**

Section 2: How Does Evolution Happen? (p. 184)

1. What is one scientific discovery that occurred during the early 1800s?

_____

_____

_____

_____

Charles Darwin (p.184)

2. Darwin's father wanted Darwin to become a

_____ , but Darwin earned a degree in

_____ instead. Later, Darwin was the

_____ on the HMS *Beagle*.

3. The Galápagos Islands are near the country of

_____ .

4. Look at Figure 14 on page 185. Describe the beak of each of the finches listed below and explain how the adaptation helps the finch find food in the Galápagos Islands.

   a. ground finch

   _____

   _____

   b. cactus finch

   _____

   _____

   c. warbler finch

   _____

   _____

Darwin Does Some Thinking (p. 186)

5. Darwin's hypothesis was that the Galápagos finches were descended from an original population of finches that was blown from South America to the Galápagos Islands.

   True or False? (Circle one.)

Chapter 8, continued

Answer these questions after reading pages 186–187. Column B lists some sources of ideas Darwin used to develop his theory of evolution. Column A lists some of the ideas that contributed to the theory. Choose the appropriate source in Column B for the idea in Column A, and write the corresponding letter in the space provided. Sources can be used more than once.

Column A	Column B
_____ **6.** The Earth was formed over a long period of time.	**a.** farmers and breeders
_____ **7.** Species can produce more offspring than can survive.	**b.** geologists
_____ **8.** Changes in animals and plants can happen in a few generations.	**c.** Thomas Malthus
_____ **9.** Selective breeding produces individuals with certain traits.	
_____ **10.** Disease and starvation affect populations.	

Natural Selection (p. 188)

11. Charles Darwin was the only scientist in the 1800s who believed the theory of evolution. True or False? (Circle one.)

12. Look at "Natural Selection in Four Steps" on page 188. What is the key to natural selection? Explain.

_____

_____

_____

_____

More Evidence of Evolution (p. 189)

13. Which of the following points was added to Darwin's theory of evolution during the 1930s and 1940s?

    a. Parents pass traits to their offspring.
    b. Variations within a species are caused by mutations.
    c. Changes in genes cannot occur.
    d. Changes in species occur over time.

Review (p. 189)

Now that you've finished Section 2, review what you learned by answering the Review questions in your ScienceLog.

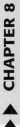

▲▶ CHAPTER 8

Section 3: Natural Selection in Action (p. 190)

1. A shorter generation time helps a population adapt

_____ . (more quickly or more slowly)

2. The microorganisms that cause some

_____ , like tuberculosis, are becoming
resistant to antibiotics.

3. After the 1850s, the _____ peppered moth
population increased because pollution altered its environment.

Formation of a New Species (p. 192)

4. List three ways that part of a population can become isolated
from the rest of the population.

_____

_____

_____

5. Separated groups may _____ to better fit
their environment over many generations.

6. Two groups of related living things are no longer considered to
be the same species when
  a. they can no longer interbreed.
  b. they do not eat the same food.
  c. they do not look the same.
  d. they become physically separated from each other.

7. After you read pages 192–193, place the following steps of specia-
tion in the correct order by writing the appropriate number in the
space provided.

_____ The populations adapt over time.

_____ The environments around the populations change.

_____ The populations become different species.

_____ Populations are divided.

Review (p. 193)

Now that you've finished Section 3, review what you learned by
answering the Review questions in you ScienceLog.

CHAPTER

9 · DIRECTED READING WORKSHEET

The History of Life on Earth

As you read Chapter 9, which begins on page 200 of your textbook, answer the following questions.

Imagine . . . (p. 200)

1. The boys were looking for a secret passage to the mansion. What did they find instead?

   _____

   _____

2. What will you learn about in this chapter?

   _____

   _____

   _____

What Do You Think? (p. 201)

Answer these questions in your ScienceLog now. Then later, you'll have a chance to revise your answers based on what you've learned.

Investigate! (p. 201)

3. In this lab, 1 cm represents

   a. 1 million years.   **c.** 100 million years.
   b. 10 million years.   **d.** 1 billion years.

Section 1: Evidence of the Past (p. 202)

4. Which of the following are true of Paul Sereno? (Circle all that apply.)

   a. He looks for fossils.   **c.** He is a police detective.
   b. He studies human history.   **d.** He is a paleontologist.

Fossils (p. 202)

5. Using Figure 2, place the following steps of fossil formation in the correct order by writing the appropriate number in the space provided.

   _____ The organism dissolves.

   _____ The organism is covered with sediment.

   _____ The hollow impression is filled with sediment.

CHAPTER 9

The Age of Fossils (p. 203)

Choose the type of fossil dating in Column B that best matches the phrase in Column A. Write the corresponding letter in the space provided. Answers in Column B may be used more than once.

Column A	Column B
____ **6.** uses sequence of rock layers	**a.** relative dating
____ **7.** gives exact age of fossils	**b.** absolute dating
____ **8.** uses ratio of stable to unstable atoms	
____ **9.** older fossils are in bottom layers of rock	
____ **10.** does not give the exact age of fossils	

11. The amount of unstable material in a rock sample

_____ as the rock sample gets older.
(increases or decreases)

Use the text and Figure 3 to mark the following statements *True* or *False*.

12. _____ All of an unstable element is gone after two half-lives.

13. _____ A half-life can be as short as a fraction of a second.

14. _____ Scientists can determine the age of a fossil by finding the age of the rock around it.

15. _____ Unstable atoms become stable atoms by releasing energy or particles or both.

The Geologic Time Scale (p. 204)

16. Scientists use the _____ to outline the history of life on Earth.

17. Look at the diagram on page 204. The _____ ,

_____ , and _____
are the periods that divide the Mesozoic era.

18. At the end of each era,
   a. new plants and animals evolved.
   b. a huge meteorite crashed into Earth.
   c. certain animals became extinct.
   d. there were no changes on Earth.

19. A species can reappear on Earth after it becomes extinct.

   True or False? (Circle one.)

20. Changes in Earth's _____ may have caused mass extinctions.

21. Land-dwelling organisms are the organisms most affected by climate changes. True or False? (Circle one.)

The Changing Earth (p. 206)

Mark the following statements *True* or *False*.

22. _____ Antarctica used to be very warm.

23. _____ Antarctica has always been at the South Pole.

24. _____ Dinosaurs once lived on Antarctica.

25. Look at Figure 5. Pangaea began to break apart

_____ years ago.

26. For what three reasons did Wegener think that all the continents used to be one continent?

a. _____

_____

b. _____

_____

c. _____

_____

27. The oceans and the _____ move on top of large pieces of the Earth's _____, called tectonic plates.

28. Over time, the motion of the continents affects the organisms that live on them. True or False? (Circle one.)

Review (p. 207)

Now that you've finished Section 1, review what you learned by answering the Review questions in your ScienceLog.

Section 2: Eras of the Geologic Time Scale (p. 208)

1. As you go down into the Grand Canyon, the rock layers get

_____ . (older or younger)

CHAPTER 9 ▲▲▲

Precambrian Time (p. 208)

2. Precambrian time continued until about

_____ years ago.

3. The early Earth had all of the following EXCEPT

    a. constant thunderstorms and volcanic eruptions.
    b. air with a high oxygen content.
    c. intense UV radiation.
    d. many meteorite strikes.

4. Scientists think that life started from a reaction that involved which of the following? (Circle all that apply.)

    a. water   **c.** dissolved minerals
    b. energy   **d.** atmospheric gases

5. Each of the following statements is false. Change the underlined word to make the statement true. Write the new word in the space provided.

    a. Prokaryotes are cells without a <u>cell wall</u>.

    _____

    b. Anaerobic organisms don't need <u>moisture</u> to survive.

    _____

    c. Figure 11 on page 210 shows <u>algae</u>, which are the simplest living organisms that photosynthesize.

    _____

6. Where did the oxygen in the Earth's atmosphere today come from?

_____

_____

_____

_____

7. _____ blocks ultraviolet radiation from the sun. (Oxygen or Ozone)

8. Plants and animals are made of _____ cells. (prokaryotic or eukaryotic)

The Paleozoic Era (p. 211)

9. Which of the following plants did not exist during the Paleozoic era?

  a. conifers   **c.** flowering plants

  b. club mosses   **d.** giant ferns

10. How did the Paleozoic era end?

_____

_____

_____

_____

The Mesozoic Era (p. 212)

11. The Mesozoic era is known as the Age of

_____ .

12. _____ appeared during the Mesozoic era. (Birds or Camels)

13. Number the steps in the theory of what caused the extinction of the dinosaurs by writing the appropriate number in the space provided.

_____ Meat-eating dinosaurs died.

_____ A large meteorite struck Earth.

_____ Plants died.

_____ Dust and smoke blocked the sunlight.

_____ Plant-eating dinosaurs died.

_____ Worldwide fires occurred.

The Cenozoic Era (p. 213)

14. We live in the Cenozoic era. True or False? (Circle one.)

15. Why do we know more about the Cenozoic era than we know about any other era?

_____

_____

_____

_____

CHAPTER 9

16. _____ are the animals that become domi-
nant during the Cenozoic era.

Review (p. 213)
Now that you've finished Section 2, review what you learned by
answering the Review questions in your ScienceLog.

Section 3: Human Evolution (p. 214)
1. Scientists think that humans share a common ancestor with

_____ and _____ .

Primates (p. 214)
2. Look at the "Characteristics of Primates" at the bottom of the
page. Primates have opposable thumbs. True or False? (Circle one.)

3. The closest living relative of humans is probably the

_____ .

4. Hominids share which of the following characteristics?
(Circle all that apply.)
  a. Hominids are bipedal.
  b. Hominids have a tilted pelvis.
  c. Hominids are primates.
  d. Hominids have a rounded jaw.

5. Look at the skeletons shown in Figure 18, on page 215. What
anatomical feature helps humans to walk upright?

_____

_____

_____

6. Hominids other than modern humans are alive today.
True or False? (Circle one.)

Hominid Evolution (p. 216)
7. Prosimians were the first _____ .

8. The australopithecines had which of the following
characteristics? (Circle all that apply.)
  a. walked on two legs
  b. had long arms
  c. had a larger brain than humans have
  d. had long legs

9. What did scientists learn about hominid evolution from Lucy?

_____

_____

_____

_____

10. Which of the following statements are true of *Homo erectus*? (Circle all that apply.)

    a. They replaced *Homo habilis*.
    b. They lived only in Africa.
    c. They hunted large animals.
    d. They built fires.
    e. They used tools made of metal.
    f. They survived for only 200,000 years.

11. What have scientists learned from studying Neanderthal camps?

_____

_____

_____

_____

12. Cro-Magnons were *Homo* _____ that had thicker and heavier bones than modern humans have.

13. Scientists today think that *Homo sapiens* evolved in

_____ from

_____ , the ancestor of all hominids.

After you have read the section about hominid evolution on pages 216–219, mark each of the following statements *True* or *False*.

14. _____ Modern humans are the only hominids who have used tools.

15. _____ The Neanderthals had a smaller brain than modern humans have.

16. _____ Modern humans have survived longer than any other hominid.

17. _____ There is not yet enough evidence to determine whether Neanderthals were a different species from modern humans.

▲▲ **CHAPTER 9**
▲▲

Choose the hominid in Column B that best matches the feature in Column A, and write the corresponding letter in the space provided.

Column A	Column B
_____ **18.** an example of a prosimian	**a.** australopithecines
_____ **19.** the most complete australopithecine skeleton ever found	**b.** Lucy
_____ **20.** the first hominids to migrate around the Earth	**c.** *Homo habilis*
_____ **21.** left footprints in Tanzania more than 3.6 million years ago	**d.** *Homo erectus*
_____ **22.** were like modern humans with heavier bones	**e.** Neanderthals
_____ **23.** lived in Europe 230,000 years ago	**f.** Cro-Magnons
_____ **24.** the first hominids with human features	**g.** lemurs

25. Figure 27 on page 219 shows two different interpretations of hominid evolution. Based on what you've learned in the chapter, which interpretation do you think is correct? Explain.

_____

_____

_____

_____

_____

Review (p. 219)

Now that you've finished Section 3, review what you learned by answering the Review questions in your ScienceLog.

CHAPTER

10 DIRECTED READING WORKSHEET

Classification

As you read Chapter 10, which begins on page 226 of your textbook, answer the following questions.

This Really Happened . . . (p. 226)

1. Why have skunks been thrown out of their family?

_____

_____

_____

_____

What Do You Think? (p. 227)

Answer these questions in your ScienceLog now. Then later, you'll have a chance to revise your answers based on what you've learned.

Investigate! (p. 227)

2. What are three characteristics of shoes that you would add to the table?

_____

_____

_____

Section 1: Classification: Sorting It All Out (p. 228)

3. Organizing plants based on whether they are poisonous or not is

   an example of classification. True or False? (Circle one.)

Why Classify? (p. 228)

4. Why do biologists classify organisms? (Circle all that apply.)

   a. to make sense of the sheer number of living things
   b. to discover how many known species there are
   c. to help study the characteristics of known species
   d. to study the relationships between species

5. What are the seven levels of classification?

_____

Chapter 10, continued

Levels of Classification (p. 229)

6. Look at Figure 2. Why do you think the bird is included in phylum Chordata but not in class Mammalia?

_____

_____

_____

What Is the Basis for Classification? (p. 230)

7. Darwin's theory of evolution didn't change the method of

classifying organisms. True or False? (Circle one.)

Choose the animal ancestor in Column B that best matches the group of animals in Column A, and write the corresponding letter in the space provided.

Column A	Column B
____ **8.** the brown bear, lion, and house cat	**a.** an ancient mammal
____ **9.** the house cat and the platypus	**b.** an ancient carnivore
____ **10.** the house cat and the lion	**c.** an ancient cat

Naming Names (p. 231)

11. In the scientific name for the Indian elephant, *Elephas maximus,*

Elephas is the _____ and *maximus* is the

_____ . Since *Tyrannosaurus rex* can be

abbreviated *T. rex, Elephas maximus* can be abbreviated

_____ .

Dichotomous Keys (p. 232)

12. After you read about dichotomous keys on page 232, look at the dichotomous key given on page 233. What type of animal has a long, nonflattened naked tail and doesn't fly?

_____

_____

Review (p. 233)

Now that you've finished Section 1, review what you learned by answering the Review questions in your ScienceLog.

Section 2: The Six Kingdoms (p. 234)

1. _____ and _____
were the only kingdoms used to classify organisms before the discovery of organisms like *Euglena,* which has characteristics of both of these kingdoms.

What Is It? (p. 234)

2. What are the characteristics of *Euglena?* (Circle all that apply.)
   a. They move around.
   b. They are multicellular.
   c. They can make their own food.
   d. They can use food from other organisms.

3. Scientists classify *Euglena* in the kingdom _____.

4. Do you think there will always be six kingdoms used for classifying organisms? Explain.

   _____

   _____

   _____

   _____

The Two Kingdoms of Bacteria (p. 235)

5. Bacteria are different from all other living things in that
   a. they are single-celled organisms.
   b. they have ribosomes.
   c. they do not have nuclei.
   d. they are microscopic.

Choose the bacteria kingdom in Column B that best matches the description in Column A, and write the corresponding letter in the space provided. The bacteria kingdoms may be used more than once.

Column A	Column B
_____ 6. live inside humans	a. Archaebacteria
_____ 7. cause pneumonia	b. Eubacteria
_____ 8. live in places where most other organisms could not survive	
_____ 9. name means "ancient"	
_____ 10. turn milk into yogurt	

CHAPTER 10

Kingdom Protista (p. 236)

11. Protists are all eukaryotic organisms that are not

_____ , _____ , or

_____ .

12. All protists are single-celled organisms. True or False?
(Circle one.)

Kingdom Plantae (p. 237)

13. Plants make sugar by using energy from the

_____ during a process called

_____ .

Kingdom Fungi (p. 238)

14. List two examples of fungi.

_____

_____

15. Fungi absorb nutrients from their surroundings
   a. through photosynthesis.
   b. after breaking them down with digestive juices.
   c. by surrounding their food and engulfing it.
   d. by eating like animals.

Kingdom Animalia (p. 239)

16. Most animals share which of the following characteristics?
(Circle all that apply.)

   a. They have a nervous system.
   b. They can move around.
   c. They photosynthesize.
   d. They are unicellular.

17. Unlike the cells of fungi, plants, most protists, and bacteria,

animal cells do not have _____ .
(cell walls or nuclei)

Review (p. 239)

Now that you've finished Section 2, review what you learned by
answering the Review questions in your ScienceLog.

CHAPTER

11 DIRECTED READING WORKSHEET

Introduction to Plants

As you read Chapter 11, which begins on page 248 of your textbook, answer the following questions.

This Really Happened . . . (p. 248)

1. What did David Noble discover in 1994?

_____

_____

_____

What Do You Think? (p. 249)

Answer these questions in your ScienceLog now. Then later, you'll have a chance to revise your answers based on what you've learned.

Investigate! (p. 249)

2. What is the purpose of this activity?

_____

_____

_____

Section 1: What Makes a Plant a Plant? (p. 250)

3. Which of the following come from plants? (Circle all that apply.)

   a. paper   **c.** a lot of food
   b. cotton   **d.** wood

Plant Characteristics (p. 250)

4. _____ are organelles that give plants their green color.

5. Chlorophyll is a _____ found in organelles

called _____ that allows plants to use

energy from the _____ to make food.

6. What does the cuticle do? (Circle all that apply.)

   a. It coats the surface of stems and leaves.
   b. It provides structural support.
   c. It helps plants retain moisture.
   d. It is an adaptation that helps plants live on dry land.

7. The cell walls of plant cells help support the plant.

True or False? (Circle one.)

Choose the word in Column B that best matches the definition in Column A, and write the corresponding letter in the space provided.

Column A	Column B
_____ **8.** tiny reproductive cells that can grow into new plants	**a.** sporophyte
_____ **9.** tiny male and female reproductive cells that join together to make a fertilized egg before they can grow into a new plant	**b.** spores
_____ **10.** stage of a plant's life during which it produces eggs and sperm cells	**c.** sex cells
_____ **11.** stage of a plant's life during which it produces spores	**d.** gametophyte

The Origin of Plants (p. 252)

12. Scientists think modern green algae and plants are descended from ancient green algae that lived in the oceans. What are two similarities between modern green algae and plants?

_____

_____

_____

_____

_____

How Are Plants Classified? (p. 252)

13. _____ plants must rely on

_____ and _____ to move substances to and from their cells because they have no pipelike tissues to transport water and nutrients.

14. Plants that have "pipelike" tissues to transport materials belong to the _____ group of plants.

Chapter 11, continued

Each of the following phrases is a characteristic of either vascular or nonvascular plants. In the space provided, write *V* for vascular plants or *N* for nonvascular plants.

15. _____ must be small

16. _____ some produce seeds

17. _____ can be any size

Choose the main group of living plants in Column B that best matches the definition in Column A, and write the corresponding letter in the space provided.

Column A	Column B
_____ **18.** vascular, seed-bearing plants with flowers	**a.** ferns, horsetails, and club mosses
_____ **19.** vascular, non-seed-bearing plants	**b.** gymnosperms
_____ **20.** nonvascular plants	**c.** mosses and liver-worts
_____ **21.** vascular, seed-bearing plants without flowers	**d.** angiosperms

Review (p. 253)

Now that you've finished Section 1, review what you learned by answering the Review questions in your ScienceLog.

Section 2: Seedless Plants (p. 254)

1. There are _____ groups of seedless plants.

Mosses and Liverworts (p. 254)

2. Why would you have a hard time finding moss growing in the hot, dry desert?

_____

_____

_____

3. Rhizoids are like roots because

  a. they contain vascular tissue.
  b. they do not contain vascular tissue.
  c. they help hold the plant in place.
  d. None of the above

Chapter 11, continued

4. During the moss life cycle, shown in Figure 7,

_____ carries the sperm cells to the egg.

5. Which of the following are true of liverworts?
(Circle all that apply.)

   a. They are nonvascular plants.
   b. They can live in very dry places.
   c. Only 60 species of liverworts exist today.
   d. Their gametophytes can be mosslike and leafy.

6. Some people might say that mosses are worth more dead than
alive. Give two examples of how this is true.

_____

_____

_____

_____

Ferns, Horsetails, and Club Mosses (p. 255)

7. The development of a vascular system allowed some ancient

plants to grow very tall. True or False? (Circle one.)

Choose the word or phrase in Column B that best matches the definition in Column A, and write the corresponding letter in the space
provided.

Column A	Column B
_____ **8.** the underground stem of most ferns	**a.** fern gametophyte
_____ **9.** produces spores	**b.** fronds
_____ **10.** wiry fern leaves and roots	**c.** fern sporophyte
_____ **11.** small heart-shaped plant that produces both sperm cells and eggs	**d.** rhizome
_____ **12.** young fern leaves	**e.** fiddleheads

13. Ferns rely on water to bring sperm cells to eggs. True or False?
(Circle one.)

14. Horsetails feel gritty because their stems contain

_____ .

15. While mosses and club mosses may look similar, only

_____ have vascular tissue.

16. Are seedless vascular plants that have been dead for 300 million years important today? Explain.

_____

_____

_____

Review (p. 257)

Now that you've finished Section 2, review what you learned by answering the Review questions in your ScienceLog.

Section 3: Plants with Seeds (p. 258)

1. _____ produce seeds in cones or fleshy structures on stems.

2. Apple trees and grasses are _____ and produce their seeds within a _____ .

Characteristics of Seed Plants (p. 258)

Mark each of the following statements *True* or *False*.

3. _____ Seeds nourish and protect young sporophytes.

4. _____ Seed plant gametophytes live independently of the sporophyte.

5. _____ The male gametophytes of seed plants need water to travel to the female gametophyte.

6. _____ The most successful plants on Earth today are seed plants.

What's So Great About Seeds? (p. 259)

7. In a seed, a young plant and _____ food are surrounded by a seed _____ .

8. Take a moment to look at the Environmental Science Connection in the right column. Why do some seeds need to be eaten to grow?

_____

_____

_____

_____

Chapter 11, continued

9. Before the young plant within the seed germinates, it already has leaves, a stem, and a small root. True or False. (Circle one.)

Gymnosperms: Seed Plants Without Flowers (p. 260)

Using the text and the photographs on page 260, choose the word in Column B that best matches the definition in Column A, and write the corresponding letter in the space provided.

Column A	Column B
_____ **10.** most are evergreens	**a.** ginkgoes
_____ **11.** group of gymnosperms that consists of very unusual plants	**b.** cycads
_____ **12.** group of gymnosperms with only one living species	**c.** conifers
_____ **13.** gymnosperms that grow in the tropics	**d.** gnetophytes

14. All conifer cones are female. True or False? (Circle one.)

Take a few minutes to look at the text and Figure 17 on page 261. Each of the following phrases describes or is an example of a sporophyte or a gametophyte of a gymnosperm. In the space provided, write *S* for a sporophyte and *G* for a gametophyte.

15. _____ a pine tree

16. _____ develops from spores

17. _____ is inside of the seed

18. _____ inside the scale of the female cone

Angiosperms: Seed Plants with Flowers (p. 262)

19. Which of the following statements is NOT true of angiosperms?

   a. They are flowering plants.
   b. There are more angiosperms than all other plant species combined.
   c. They produce seeds within fruits.
   d. They are nonvascular plants.

20. Flowers rely on _____ that may carry pollen from flower to flower.

21. The main function of a fruit is to protect seeds.

   True or False? (Circle one.)

22. Seeds don't have legs, but they sure get around! Give two examples of how seeds are transported to new areas.

_____

_____

_____

_____

_____

_____

Take a look at the text and Figure 20 on page 263. Each of the following phrases describes or is an example of either a monocot or a dicot. In the space provided, write *M* for a monocot and *D* for a dicot.

23. _____ has one seed leaf

24. _____ an onion

25. _____ has leaves with branching veins

26. _____ flower parts are in threes

27. _____ vascular tissue is in a ring

28. _____ flower parts are in fours or fives

29. Which of the following come from flowering plants? (Circle all that apply.)

   a. food crops   **c.** rubber
   b. perfume oils   **d.** clothing fibers

Review (p. 263)

Now that you've finished Section 3, review what you learned by answering the Review questions in your ScienceLog.

Section 4: The Structures of Seed Plants (p. 264)

1. What do you have in common with plants?

_____

_____

_____

_____

Plant Systems (p. 264)

Mark each of the following statements *True* or *False*.

2. _____ The shoot system is made up of stems.

3. _____ The root system and shoot system work independently of each other.

4. _____ Xylem is a vascular tissue that transports water and minerals through a plant.

5. _____ Sugar is transported by the phloem.

The Root of the Matter (p. 264)

6. Which of the following is NOT one of the main functions of roots?

   a. supplying plants with water and minerals from the soil
   b. making food through photosynthesis
   c. supporting and anchoring the plant
   d. storing food as sugar or starch

7. Roots have root hairs. What do root hairs do?

_____

_____

_____

_____

8. The slimy substance produced by the root cap

   a. protects the tip of the root.
   b. attracts minerals in the soil.
   c. helps water diffuse through the root's epidermis.
   d. helps the root grow through soil.

9. _____ obtain water from deep underground, while _____ roots obtain water close to the surface of the soil.

What's the Holdup? (p. 266)

Mark each of the following statements *True* or *False*.

10. _____ Stems are always located above the ground.

11. _____ Stems connect the roots to the leaves and flowers.

12. _____ Stems display flowers to pollinators.

13. _____ Stems can store water.

Chapter 11, continued

Stem Structures (p. 267)

14. Poppies and clovers have herbaceous stems that are soft, thin, and flexible. True or False? (Circle one.)

15. What do a tree's growth rings have to do with xylem?

_____

_____

_____

_____

_____

Review (p. 267)

Now that you've finished the first part of Section 4, review what you learned by answering the Review questions in your ScienceLog.

A Plant's Food Factories (p. 268)

16. What are a plant's food factories? Explain.

_____

_____

_____

Choose the term in Column B that best matches the definition in Column A, and write the corresponding letter in the space provided.

Column A	Column B
_____ **17.** cells that open and close the stomata	**a.** stoma
_____ **18.** layer of cells that contains many chloroplasts	**b.** guard cells
_____ **19.** a single layer of cells that covers the top and bottom surfaces of a leaf	**c.** spongy layer
_____ **20.** a tiny pore that allows carbon dioxide to enter the leaf	**d.** epidermis
_____ **21.** contains air spaces between the cells that allow carbon dioxide to diffuse freely	**e.** palisade layer
_____ **22.** contain xylem and phloem surrounded by supporting tissue	**f.** veins

23. Cactus spines are leaves. True or False? (Circle one.)

24. Figure 28 in the right-hand column of page 269 shows an insect caught on the special leaves of a sundew. How does catching insects enable the sundew to live in its environment?

_____

_____

_____

_____

Flowers (p. 270)

Mark each of the following statements *True* or *False*.

25. _____ Flowers are adaptations for sexual reproduction.

26. _____ Sepals protect the mature flower.

27. _____ Petals may attract animals to the flower.

28. The _____ in a flower produce pollen.

29. The pistil of a flower includes the _____,

style, and _____ .

30. The eggs of a flower are found in the

_____ .

31. If the egg is fertilized, what part of the flower develops into a fruit?

_____

_____

32. All flowers have brightly colored petals to attract insects.

True or False? (Circle one.)

Review (p. 271)

Now that you've finished Section 4, review what you learned by answering the Review questions in your ScienceLog.

CHAPTER

12   DIRECTED READING WORKSHEET

Plant Processes

As you read Chapter 12, which begins on page 278 of your textbook, answer the following questions.

Strange but True! (p. 278)

1. How do wasps act as a natural pesticide for corn plants?

_____

_____

_____

_____

What Do You Think? (p. 279)

Answer these questions in your ScienceLog now. Then later, you'll have a chance to revise your answers based on what you've learned.

Investigate! (p. 279)

2. What is the purpose of this activity?

_____

_____

_____

Section 1: The Reproduction of Flowering Plants (p. 280)

3. Which of the following statements is NOT true of flowering plants?

  a. Fertilization takes place within the flower.
  b. They produce seeds in fruit.
  c. They use flowers to reproduce asexually.
  d. They are the largest group of plants in the world.

How Does Fertilization Occur? (p. 280)

4. Flowers can have both male and female reproductive structures.

  True or False? (Circle one.)

5. Number the following steps of flower fertilization in the order of their occurrence by writing the appropriate number in the space provided.

_____ Pollen lands on the stigma.

_____ A sperm cell fuses with an egg in the ovule.

_____ A pollen tube grows down through the style to the ovary.

Use Figure 1 to answer the following questions.

6. Each ovule contains an egg. True or False? (Circle one.)

7. The ovary contains pollen. True or False? (Circle one.)

From Flower to Fruit (p. 281)

8. The ovule becomes a _____ after fertilization.

Familiar Fruits (p. 282)

9. A fruit, which protects and holds the seeds, develops from the

_____ of a flower.

Seeds Become New Plants (p. 282)

10. The root of the word *dormant* means "to sleep." Why is this word used to describe many seeds?

_____

_____

_____

11. Which of the following are minimum requirements needed for seeds to sprout? (Circle all that apply.)

a. water   c. oxygen
b. sunlight   d. a suitable temperature

Other Methods of Reproduction (p. 283)

12. Can a strawberry plant, like the one shown in Figure 4, reproduce without flowers? Explain.

_____

_____

Review (p. 283)

Now that you've finished Section 1, review what you learned by answering the Review questions in your ScienceLog.

_____

Section 2: The Ins and Outs of Making Food (p. 284)

1. Plants use the gas _____ to make their own food.

What Happens During Photosynthesis (p. 284)

2. Chloroplasts are _____; chlorophyll is a(n)

   _____. (pigments or organelles, pigment or organelle)

3. Green light is reflected by chlorophyll. True or False? (Circle one.)

4. During photosynthesis, light energy is used to split water into

   _____ and _____.

5. Sugar is broken down by plant cells for energy during cellular respiration. True or False? (Circle one.)

Gas Exchange (p. 286)

6. The openings in the _____ and cuticle of a leaf, called stomata, are surrounded by two

   _____, which open and close the gap.

7. Look at Figure 7. Why are stomata usually closed when it is dark?

   _____

   _____

   _____

   _____

8. Transpiration is the loss of water vapor from leaves.

   True or False? (Circle one.)

9. Which of the following does NOT occur through open stomata?
   a. water entering the leaf
   b. oxygen leaving the leaf
   c. carbon dioxide entering the leaf
   d. transpiration

Review (p. 286)

Now that you've finished Section 2, review what you learned by answering the Review questions in your ScienceLog.

CHAPTER 12

Section 3: Plant Responses to the Environment (p. 287)

1. Unlike humans, plants cannot respond to changes in their environment. True or False? (Circle one.)

Plant Tropisms (p. 287)

2. When a tropism is _____, a plant will grow toward the stimulus. (positive or negative)

3. The shoot tips of a plant exhibit positive phototropism. True or False? (Circle one.)

4. Take a look at Figure 9. How does a plant bend?

_____

_____

_____

_____

5. In plants, most _____ tips have positive gravitropism, while most _____ tips have negative gravitropism.

6. Why do the shoots of the plants in Figure 10, on page 288, have such unusual shapes?

_____

_____

_____

_____

_____

Seasonal Responses (p. 289)

7. Plants can detect when the seasons change. True or False? (Circle one.)

8. Look at the Earth Science Connection in the right column of page 289. When the Northern Hemisphere is tilted toward the sun, it is _____ in the Northern Hemisphere. (summer or winter)

Chapter 12, continued

Each of the following statements is true of either short-day plants or long-day plants. In the space provided, write *S* if it is true of short-day plants and *L* if it is true of long-day plants.

9. _____ Ragweed is an example.

10. _____ They flower in spring or early summer.

11. _____ They flower in late summer or early autumn.

12. _____ They flower when the night length is short.

13. The poinsettias in Figure 11
   a. flower when the nights are long.
   b. are all green when the nights are long.
   c. flower in the early summer.
   d. do not flower in the fall.

14. Even evergreen trees lose their leaves. True or False? (Circle one.)

15. In tropical climates that have wet and dry seasons, deciduous trees
   a. lose their leaves when winter begins.
   b. lose their leaves when the dry season begins.
   c. lose their leaves when the wet season begins.
   d. never lose their leaves.

16. Why do tree leaves change color in the fall?

_____

_____

_____

_____

Review (p. 291)

Now that you've finished Section 3, review what you learned by answering the Review questions in your ScienceLog.

Section 4: Plant Growth (p. 292)

1. A plant's _____ ,

_____ , and _____

affect its growth.

Heredity (p. 292)

2. A plant's traits are determined by heredity. True or False? (Circle one.)

CHAPTER 12

Environment (p. 292)

3. The plants in Figure 14 have identical genes. How do they look different, and why?

_____

_____

_____

_____

4. The following are all examples of environmental factors that can affect plant growth EXCEPT

   a. the amount of daylight and darkness.

   b. the water availability.

   c. the plant's characteristics.

   d. the soil composition.

Plant Hormones (p. 293)

5. Auxin is a growth hormone in plants that

   a. travels to the lighted side of the plant stem.

   b. causes plants to grow toward light.

   c. is produced in fruits.

   d. causes plant cells to shrink.

6. Why do farmers sometimes spray gibberellin on grape stems?

_____

_____

_____

_____

Review (p. 293)

Now that you've finished Section 4, review what you learned by answering the Review questions in your ScienceLog.

CHAPTER

13   DIRECTED READING WORKSHEET

Animals and Behavior

As you read Chapter 13, which begins on page 302 of your textbook, answer the following questions.

This Really Happened . . . (p. 302)

1a. What did Ridgely and Navarette hear while they were hiking in the mountains?

_____

_____

b. What did the answer to (a) sound like?

_____

_____

2. The bird Navarette and Ridgely discovered

    a. has a long tail.   **c.** has short legs.

    b. eats seeds.   **d.** does not have a name yet.

What Do You Think? (p. 303)

Answer these questions in your ScienceLog now. Then later, you'll have a chance to revise your answers based on what you've learned.

Investigate! (p. 303)

3. What is the purpose of this activity?

_____

_____

_____

Section 1: What Is an Animal? (p. 304)

4. Natural bath sponges used to be living plants. True or False? (Circle one.)

5. Describe the smallest animal you've ever seen.

_____

_____

_____

▲ ▲ CHAPTER 13

The Animal Kingdom (p. 304)

6. Which of the following lists contains types of organisms that are NOT animals?

    a. corals, birds, kangaroos
    b. dolphins, cactuses, whales
    c. spiders, humans, sponges
    d. sea anemones, fish, slugs

Use Figure 3 to determine whether each of the following types of animals is an invertebrate or a vertebrate. In the space provided, write *I* if it is an invertebrate and *V* if it is a vertebrate.

7. _____ beetles

8. _____ mammals

9. _____ worms

10. _____ spiders

That's an Animal? (p. 305)

Mark each of the following statements *True* or *False*.

11. _____ All animals are multicellular.

12. _____ Animal cells are prokaryotic.

13. _____ Some animals can reproduce asexually.

14. In the _____ stage of its development, an organism is called an embryo.

15. Which of the following specialized parts are organs? (Circle all that apply.)

    a. muscles   c. heart
    b. kidneys   d. nerves

16. Animals are the only organisms that can move. True or False? (Circle one.)

17. Plants can make their own food, but animals cannot. How do animals survive?

    _____

    _____

    _____

Review (p. 307)

Now that you've finished Section 1, review what you learned by answering the Review questions in your ScienceLog.

Section 2: Animal Behavior (p. 308)

1. The activities that animals perform, such as building homes and stalking food, are called _____ .

Survival Behavior (p. 308)

2. Survival behaviors help animals find food, water, and a place to live, and help them avoid being eaten. True or False? (Circle one.)

3. Animals use different methods in order to obtain the

   most _____ for the least amount of

   _____ .

4. Predators hunt and eat other _____ , called prey.

5. Use the text to give one example of an animal that uses camouflage.

   _____

   _____

   _____

6. How does the hooded pitohui bird defend itself from predators?
   a. Its bite injects a powerful acid into its attacker.
   b. It is covered in spines.
   c. It can spray a chemical that smells very bad.
   d. Its skin contains a toxin that can kill a predator.

7. Warning coloration is helpful to prey because it keeps prey from being eaten. Why is warning coloration sometimes helpful to predators?

   _____

   _____

   _____

Why Do They Behave That Way? (p. 310)

8. Animals always know instinctively what to do. True or False? (Circle one.)

9. Innate behaviors are influenced by _____

   and do not depend on experience or _____ .

10. Innate behavior cannot be changed. True or False? (Circle one.)

11. The tendency of humans to speak is a(n)

_____ behavior but the language we

speak is a(n) _____ behavior.

Review (p. 310)
Now that you've finished the first part of Section 2, review what you
learned by answering the Review questions in your ScienceLog.

Seasonal Behavior (p. 311)
12. What are two ways animals deal with winter?

_____

_____

_____

13. The only reason animals travel from one place to another and

back again is to find food and water. True or False? (Circle one.)

14. Which of the following does NOT happen during hibernation?
   a. The animal's heart rate drops.
   b. The animal survives on stored body fat.
   c. The animal's temperature increases.
   d. The animal does not wake for weeks at a time.

15. Sometimes desert animals experience an internal slowdown

during the summer. True or False? (Circle one.)

The Rhythms of Life (p. 312)
16. To set their biological clock, animals use clues such as the

_____ of the _____

and the _____ .

17. Circadian rhythms are daily cycles. What is an example of a
circadian rhythm?

_____

_____

How Do Animals Find Their Way? (p. 312)
18. Arctic terns have to _____ to make their
38,000 km round trip.

19. All of the landmarks that animals use to navigate are things that

they can see, such as mountains and rivers. True or False?
(Circle one.)

20. Look at the Physical Science Connection on page 313. Migratory
birds have crystals of a mineral called magnetite above their nos-
trils. How do scientists think this mineral helps them?

_____

_____

_____

Review (p. 313)

Now that you've finished Section 2, review what you learned by
answering the Review questions in your ScienceLog.

Section 3: Living Together (p. 314)

1. The _____ between animals of the same
species requires communication.

Communication (p. 314)

2. What two things must happen for communication to occur
between two animals?

_____

_____

_____

_____

3. Why are the cranes in Figure 17 dancing?
   a. They are telling each other where to find food.
   b. The dance leads to mating.
   c. They are frightening away predators.
   d. They are warning each other of danger.

4. The wolves in Figure 18 are howling to defend their living space

from other wolves. True or False? (Circle one.)

How Do Animals Communicate? (p. 315)

5. Animals use their senses, such as sight and touch, to convey

_____ information.

CHAPTER 13

Chapter 13, continued

6. Which of the following messages do ants communicate using pheromones? (Circle all that apply.)

   a. Danger!   **c.** Follow me!
   b. I'm from your colony. **d.** I'm your friend.

7. Insects use some of the same pheromones to attract mates that

   elephants use. True or False? (Circle one.)

Match the noise in Column B with the type of animal that uses that noise for communication in Column A, and write the corresponding letter in the space provided.

Column A	Column B
____ **8.** elephants	**a.** songs
____ **9.** male birds	**b.** low rumbles
____ **10.** dolphins	**c.** howls
____ **11.** wolves	**d.** complex clicks

12. Fireflies blinking and humans winking are both examples

    of communication. True or False? (Circle one.)

13. Look at the diagram on page 316. If you were a honeybee, how would learning the waggle dance help you find food?

    _____

    _____

    _____

Part of the Family (p. 317)

14. Look at the ground squirrel in Figure 23. What is one benefit and one downside to living in a group?

    _____

    _____

    _____

    _____

Review (p. 317)

Now that you've finished Section 3, review what you learned by answering the Review questions in your ScienceLog.

CHAPTER
14 DIRECTED READING WORKSHEET

Invertebrates

As you read Chapter 14, which begins on page 324 of your textbook, answer the following questions.

Amazing but True! (p. 324)

1. What does the giant leech pictured on page 324 have to do with people with spinal cord injuries?

_____

_____

_____

_____

_____

2. Leeches and all the other animals in this chapter do not have a

_____ .

What Do You Think? (p. 325)

Answer these questions in your ScienceLog now. Then later, you'll have a chance to revise your answers based on what you've learned.

Investigate! (p. 325)

3. What is the purpose of this activity?

_____

_____

Section 1: Simple Invertebrates (p. 326)

4. There are more humans than invertebrates on Earth.

   True or False? (Circle one.)

No Backbones Here! (p. 326)

5. List three features scientists use to compare different animals.

_____

_____

_____

_____

CHAPTER 14

Chapter 14, continued

In the space provided, write *B* if the animal has bilateral symmetry, *R* if the animal has radial symmetry, or *A* if the animal is asymmetrical. To see a picture of each animal, look at pages 325, 326, 327, and 345 in your text.

6. _____ sea star

7. _____ crab

8. _____ sponge

9. _____ butterfly

10. A _____ is a control center for the entire body, while a _____ controls only the functions near its location. (ganglion or brain, ganglion or brain)

11. The coelom and the gut are both digestive organs.

True or False? (Circle one.)

12. In animals without a coelom, moving from one place to another can aid or hinder digestion. True or False? (Circle one.)

Sponges (p. 328)

13. Is a sponge considered an animal? Explain.

_____

_____

_____

14. Sponge skeletons are made of _____ ,

_____ , or _____ .

15. Can you kill a sponge by breaking it into pieces? Explain.

_____

_____

_____

16. What physical characteristic of a sponge does the name Porifera suggest?

_____

_____

17. Why doesn't the sponge need to have a gut?

_____

_____

Review (p. 329)

Now that you've finished the first part of Section 1, review what you learned by answering the Review questions in your ScienceLog.

Cnidarians (p. 330)

18. Which of the following are true about cnidarians? (Circle all that apply.)

    a. They have stinging cells, which they use to hunt.
    b. They can regenerate lost body parts.
    c. They live only in fresh water.
    d. They include sponges, corals, and hydras.

19. Cnidarians are either in _____ form or in

_____ form. Both body types have

_____ symmetry.

20. The sea anemone is a polyp. True or False? (Circle one.)

21. A cnidarian will always have the same body form for its entire

life. True or False? (Circle one.)

22. All cnidarians have a nerve _____, which controls movement of the body and tentacles.

23. Jellyfish have a nerve _____, which coordinates swimming.

Flatworms (p. 332)

24. Which of the following does NOT describe flatworms?

    a. They have a head.
    b. They are radially symmetric.
    c. They have eyespots and sensory lobes.
    d. They have a brain.

25. Flukes and tapeworms can live inside or outside a host.

True or False? (Circle one.)

▲▲ **CHAPTER 14**

26. Like all tapeworms, the tapeworm on page 333 has no

_____ , _____ ,

or _____ .

Roundworms (p. 333)

27. How is the digestive system of a roundworm different from the digestive system of a planarian?

_____

_____

_____

28. Which of the following meats could give you trichinosis if it is infected and you don't cook it thoroughly?

    a. chicken   **c.** steak

    b. pork   **d.** fish

Review (p. 333)

Now that you've finished Section 1, review what you learned by answering the Review questions in your ScienceLog.

Section 2: Mollusks and Annelid Worms (p. 334)

1. What features of mollusks make them more sophisticated organisms than roundworms, flatworms, and corals?

_____

_____

Mollusks (p. 334)

2. Which of the three main classes of mollusks are you most likely to encounter on land?

_____

_____

3. Which of the following are true of the phylum Mollusca? (Circle all that apply.)

    a. Some mollusks are 1 mm in length.

    b. Some mollusks are 18 m in length.

    c. Some land mollusks can move 40 km/h.

    d. Some marine mollusks can swim 40 km/h.

Name _____ Date _____ Class _____

Chapter 14, continued

Choose the part of the mollusk in Column B that best matches the definition in Column A, and write the corresponding letter in the space provided.

Column A	Column B
____ **4.** a layer of tissue that protects mollusks that do not have a shell	**a.** shell
____ **5.** this contains the gills, gut, and other organs	**b.** mantle
____ **6.** this keeps land mollusks from drying out	**c.** foot
____ **7.** mollusks use this to move	**d.** visceral mass

8. Snails and slugs have a _____ to scrape food off rocks.

9. How are open and closed circulatory systems different?

    a. Open circulatory systems have sinuses.
    b. Closed circulatory systems have sinuses.
    c. Only open circulatory systems have blood vessels.
    d. Only closed circulatory systems have blood vessels.

10. Octopuses have advanced nervous systems. Name two examples of difficult tasks that some octopuses can do.

_____

_____

_____

Review (p. 336)

Now that you've finished the first part of Section 2, review what you learned by answering the Review questions in your ScienceLog.

Annelid Worms (p. 337)

11. An earthworm has a brain. True or False? (Circle one.)

12. All the segments of an annelid worm are identical.

    True or False? (Circle one.)

13. How do earthworms increase soil fertility? (Circle all that apply.)

    a. They eat bugs that poison the soil.
    b. Their excreted wastes provide nutrients to plants.
    c. They burrow tunnels that allow water and air to reach deep into the soil.
    d. They have bristles that protect plant roots.

14. What does the bristle worm in Figure 19 use its bristles to do?

    a. burrow   **c.** deter predators

    b. filter food out of water   **d.** protect itself from drying out

15. How can leeches help sick people?

_____

_____

_____

Review (p. 338)

Now that you've finished Section 2, review what you learned by answering the Review questions in your ScienceLog.

Section 3: Arthropods (p. 339)

1. Which of the following invertebrates is NOT an arthropod?

    a. a crab   **c.** a centipede

    b. a spider   **d.** a sea urchin

Characteristics of Arthropods (p. 339)

2. Why are jointed limbs important to an arthropod?

_____

_____

_____

3. The "suit of armor" that arthropods wear is called a(n)

_____, which is made of

_____ .

Kinds of Arthropods (p. 340)

4. The difference between a centipede and a millipede is that a

millipede has _____ pairs of legs per

segment, while a centipede has _____

pair(s). (two or three, one or two)

5. All crustaceans have _____ and two pairs

of _____ .

(legs or mandibles, antennae or eyes)

6. Ticks and mites are types of insects. True or False? (Circle one.)

Chapter 14, continued

7. Why are insects important to us?

_____

_____

_____

Read pages 340–343 before answering questions 8–15. Match each type of arthropod in Column B to the correct statement in Column A, and write the corresponding letter in the appropriate space. Arthropod types can be used more than once.

Column A	Column B
_____ **8.** has eight eyes	**a.** arachnid
_____ **9.** has simple eyes	**b.** insect
_____ **10.** has compound eyes	
_____ **11.** has two main body parts	
_____ **12.** has three main body parts	
_____ **13.** has antennae	
_____ **14.** has mandibles	
_____ **15.** has chelicerae	

Look at the diagram on page 344. Place the following stages of complete metamorphosis in order by writing the appropriate number in the space provided.

16. _____ pupa

17. _____ larva

18. _____ egg

19. _____ adult

Review (p. 344)

Now that you've finished Section 3, review what you learned by answering the Review questions in your ScienceLog.

Section 4: Echinoderms (p. 345)

1. If you went snorkeling in a freshwater lake, would you see any echinoderms? Why or why not?

_____

_____

Spiny Skinned (p. 345)

2. How do echinoderms use their endoskeleton like an exoskeleton?

_____

_____

_____

3. An endoskeleton is covered by an outer skin, while a true

exoskeleton has no covering. True or False? (Circle one.)

Bilateral or Radial? (p. 345)

4. Most echinoderms begin their life with

_____ symmetry and later have

_____ symmetry.

The Nervous System (p. 346)

5. Which sense does a sea star have?

   a. smell   **c.** hearing

   b. sight   **d.** taste

6. A sea star has a circle of nerve fibers around its

_____ called a nerve ring. (mouth or arms)

Water Vascular System (p. 346)

7. Which of the following is NOT part of the water vascular system?

   a. ampulla   **c.** sieve plate

   b. radial canals   **d.** radial nerve

8. Tube feet help a starfish to capture food and hang onto rocks.

True or False? (Circle one.)

Kinds of Echinoderms (p. 347)

9. Besides using their tube feet how else do sea urchins get around?

_____

_____

Review (p. 347)

Now that you've finished Section 4, review what you learned by answering the Review questions in your ScienceLog.

15 DIRECTED READING WORKSHEET

Fishes, Amphibians, and Reptiles

As you read Chapter 15, which begins on page 354 of your textbook, answer the following questions.

Would You Believe . . . ? (p. 354)

1. What was so amazing about Marjorie Courtenay Latimer's discovery?

_____

_____

_____

What Do You Think? (p. 355)

Answer these questions in your ScienceLog now. Then later, you'll have a chance to revise your answers based on what you've learned.

Investigate! (p. 355)

2. Birds and modern _____ have eggs with

_____ .

Section 1: What Are Vertebrates? (p. 356)

3. What does a dinosaur skeleton have in common with your skeleton?

_____

_____

_____

Chordates (p. 356)

Mark each of the following statements *True* or *False*.

4. _____ Animals with a backbone belong to the phylum Chordata.

5. _____ The largest group of chordates are vertebrates.

6. _____ Lancelets do not have a backbone and therefore are not true chordates.

7. _____ An organism must have all four of the special chordate body parts as an adult in order to belong to the phylum Chordata.

Chapter 15, continued

Use Figure 3 on page 357 to choose the term in Column B that best matches the definition in Column A. Then write the corresponding letter in the space provided.

Column A	Column B
_____ **8.** In vertebrates this structure is filled with spinal fluid.	**a.** notochord
_____ **9.** This structure is located behind the anus.	**b.** pharyngeal pouch
_____ **10.** In most vertebrates this structure disappears and a backbone grows in its place.	**c.** tail
_____ **11.** This structure develops into a gill or other body part as an embryo matures.	**d.** hollow nerve cord

Getting a Backbone (p. 357)

12. Vertebrates are different from other chordates because

    a. tunicates and lancelets have pharyngeal pouches.
    b. they have a notochord.
    c. they do not have a postanal tail.
    d. they have a backbone and a skull.

13. A segmented column of bones called

_____ protects the nerve cord, and a

_____ protects the head.

14. The name of the tough material in the flexible parts of your nose and ears is called cartilage. True or False? (Circle one.)

15. Why do you think we know more about the evolution of vertebrates than any other group of organisms?

_____

_____

_____

_____

_____

Are Vertebrates Warm or Cold? (p. 358)

16. There is an ideal temperature range for the chemical reactions that take place inside an animal's body cells. True or False? (Circle one.)

17. How does an endotherm stay warm when it's cold outside?

_____

_____

_____

18. An endotherm's body temperature _____
when the temperature of the environment changes.
(changes a lot or stays about the same)

19. Which of the following statements is NOT true?

    a. Ectotherms include most fish, amphibians, and reptiles.
    b. Ectotherms' body temperature does not fluctuate.
    c. Ectotherms can have cool or warm blood.
    d. Ectotherms are sometimes called "coldblooded."

Review (p. 358)

Now that you've finished Section 1, review what you learned by
answering the Review questions in your ScienceLog.

Section 2: Fishes (p. 359)

1. Which of the following statements is NOT true?

    a. Fish can live almost anywhere except in cold arctic waters.
    b. The first vertebrates appeared about 500 million years ago.
    c. There are more species of fishes today than all other vertebrates
       combined.
    d. More than 25,000 species of fishes exist.

2. Take a look at the fishes in Figure 7. Why do you think a seahorse
is considered a fish?

_____

_____

_____

Fish Characteristics (p. 359)

3. What parts of a fish's body help the fish move, steer, stop, and
balance?

_____

_____

4. The lateral line system in fish enables them to keep track of
information. True or False? (Circle one.)

5. How do fish use their gills to breathe?

_____

_____

_____

_____

6. In external fertilization, the male fish drops sperm onto the unfertilized eggs in the water. True or False? (Circle one.)

7. After internal fertilization takes place, fish always give birth to live young. True or False? (Circle one.)

Types of Fishes (p. 361)

8. There are _____ different classes of fishes alive today. Two other classes of fishes are now

_____ .

9. Which is NOT true of jawless fishes?
   a. They are eel-like.
   b. They have backbones.
   c. They have round mouths.
   d. They were the first fishes.

10. The skeleton of a cartilaginous fish, such as a ray, never changes from cartilage to bone. True or False? (Circle one.)

11. A cartilaginous fish has a jaw and is an expert

_____ .

12. How can a shark's skin hurt you?

_____

_____

_____

13. In order to stay afloat, a cartilaginous fish stores oil in its

_____ and keeps swimming.

14. How does a cartilaginous fish keep from suffocating?
   (Circle all that apply.)
   a. It keeps swimming.   **c.** It pumps water across its gills.
   b. It goes to the surface for air. **d.** It swims at certain depths.

15. All bony fishes have a _____ made of bone instead of cartilage.

16. Bony fishes have a body covered by scales. True or False? (Circle one.)

17. Which is NOT true of a swim bladder?

    a. It's found in bony fishes.
    b. It's filled with gases from the bloodstream.
    c. It gives the fish buoyancy.
    d. It helps fishes steer against wave action.

18. Most bony fishes are _____-finned fishes.

19. _____-finned fishes, such as coelacanths, have thick, muscular fins.

20. Lungfishes, like the one shown in Figure 16 at the bottom of page 363, can gulp air. True or False? (Circle one.)

Review (p. 363)

Now that you've finished Section 2, review what you learned by answering the Review questions in your ScienceLog.

Section 3: Amphibians (p. 364)

1. 350 million years ago, what made the land such a wonderful place for vertebrates?

_____

_____

Moving to Land (p. 364)

2. The lungs of lungfishes became an adaptation for walking.

    True or False? (Circle one.)

3. What did the first amphibians look like?

_____

_____

4. Early amphibians needed to return to the water from time to

    time. True or False? (Circle one.)

CHAPTER 15

Characteristics of Amphibians (p. 365)

5. How do amphibians lead a "double-life"?

_____

_____

_____

_____

_____

Mark each of the following statements *True* or *False*.

6. _____ Amphibians do not drink water.

7. _____ An amphibian's skin makes it easy for the animal to become dehydrated.

8. _____ Some amphibians breathe only through their skin.

9. _____ All amphibians with brightly colored skin are deadly.

10. Amphibian embryos must develop in a wet environment because

    a. their eggs lack shells.
    b. they begin life as fish.
    c. they are ectotherms.
    d. the water is less polluted than the air.

11. When an amphibian goes through _____,
it changes from its larval form, a tadpole, into its adult form.

12. Where does the embryo of the Darwin frog finish developing?

_____

_____

Kinds of Amphibians (p. 367)

13. Frogs and toads belong to the same group of amphibians.

    True or False? (Circle one.)

14. How are caecilians different from most other amphibians?
(Circle all that apply.)

    a. They don't have legs.
    b. Some have bony scales.
    c. They are shaped like snakes.
    d. They have thin, moist skin.

15. How are salamanders similar to their prehistoric amphibian ancestors?

_____

_____

16. A good place to look for a salamander in North America is under a

_____ or a _____ .

17. All salamanders go through metamorphosis. True or False? (Circle one.)

18. Frogs and toads are found only in temperate parts of the world.

True or False? (Circle one.)

Use the information on page 368 to mark each of the following phrases *F* if it is characteristic of a frog, *T* if it is characteristic of a toad, or *B* if it is characteristic of both a frog and a toad.

19. _____ extendible, sticky tongue

20. _____ dry, bumpy skin

21. _____ spends more time in the water

22. _____ has less webbing in its feet

23. _____ powerful leg muscles

24. _____ shorter hind legs

25. _____ moist skin

26. Frogs have a special structure called a vocal sac that humans don't have. What does this structure do?

_____

_____

_____

_____

Review (p. 368)

Now that you've finished Section 3, review what you learned by answering the Review questions in your ScienceLog.

Section 4: Reptiles (p. 369)

1. After _____ years, some amphibians evolved into animals that could live on dry land.

2. Which of the following traits allowed the first reptiles to live completely out of the water? (Circle all that apply.)

    a. an egg that could be laid on dry land

    b. stronger, more vertical legs

    c. thick, dry skin

    d. teeth

Reptile History (p. 369)

3. Some prehistoric reptiles could fly. True or False? (Circle one.)

4. Mammals had reptile ancestors called _____ that are now extinct.

Characteristics of Reptiles (p. 370)

5. How is a reptile's skin an important adaptation for life on land?

_____

_____

_____

_____

6. Reptiles are less active when the environment is _____ and more active when the environment is _____ .

7. Most reptiles live in mild climates because they usually cannot maintain a constant body temperature. True or False? (Circle one.)

8. What are the advantages of an amniotic egg?

_____

_____

_____

_____

Chapter 15, continued

Choose the part of the amniotic egg in Column B that best matches the definition in Column A, and write the corresponding letter in the space provided.

Column A	Column B
____ **9.** supplies the embryo with food	**a.** yolk
____ **10.** stores waste from the embryo and passes oxygen to the embryo	**b.** albumen
____ **11.** keeps the egg from drying out	**c.** amniotic sac
____ **12.** fluid-filled structure that protects the embryo from injury	**d.** allantois
____ **13.** provides the embryo with protein and water	**e.** shell

14. Which of the following are true of reptiles? (Circle all that apply.)
  a. Reptiles don't undergo metamorphosis.
  b. Reptile embryos develop directly into tiny reptiles.
  c. All reptiles lay eggs.
  d. Reptiles don't have a larval stage.

Types of Reptiles (p. 371)

15. Most of the reptiles that have ever lived are now

_____ .

16. List the three groups of modern reptiles.

_____

_____

17. Which of the following is NOT true of both turtles and tortoises?
  a. They are only distantly related to the other reptiles.
  b. They spend some or all of their lives in the water.
  c. Their armorlike shells protect them from predators.
  d. They are slow and inflexible.

18. All crocodiles and alligators are _____ . (carnivores or herbivores)

19. In Figure 34 at the bottom of page 372, how can you tell the difference between a crocodile and an alligator?

_____

_____

Mark each of the following statements *True* or *False*.

20. _____ Lizards include skinks, chameleons, alligators, and geckos.

21. _____ On rare occasions, the largest lizards, one of which is shown in Figure 35, have been known to eat humans.

22. _____ Snakes move on smooth surfaces by using suckers on their bellies to grip the surface and pull forward.

23. _____ Snakes are not herbivores.

24. _____ Snakes have special, five-jointed jaws that allow them to swallow their prey whole.

25. _____ Snakes have an acute sense of hearing.

26. How does a snake use its tongue to smell?

_____

_____

_____

_____

_____

_____

Review (p. 373)

Now that you've finished Section 4, review what you've learned by answering the Review questions in your ScienceLog.

CHAPTER
16   **DIRECTED READING WORKSHEET**

Birds and Mammals

As you read Chapter 16, which begins on page 380 of your textbook, answer the following questions.

Would You Believe . . . ? (p. 380)

1. What evidence did Chinese scientists find in 1998 that dinosaurs are related to pigeons?

_____

_____

2. Some scientists think that dinosaurs did not become extinct

because birds are dinosaurs. True or False? (Circle one.)

What Do You Think? (p. 381)

Answer these questions in your ScienceLog now. Then later, you'll have a chance to revise your answers based on what you've learned.

Investigate! (p. 381)

3. What is the purpose of this experiment?

_____

_____

Section 1: Birds (p. 382)

4. If a living animal has _____ , it's a bird.

Bird Characteristics (p. 382)

5. Which of the following characteristics do birds share with modern-day reptiles? (Circle all that apply.)

   a. thick, dry scales on their legs and feet
   b. vertebrae
   c. amniotic egg
   d. hard eggshells

6. When bird feathers get old, they fall out, and new feathers grow in

their place. True or False? (Circle one.)

7. Down feathers help keep birds from losing

_____ .

8. The main function of contour feathers is to

    a. form a streamlined flying surface.

    b. attract a mate.

    c. provide protection.

    d. provide warmth.

9. How does preening make a bird's feathers water-repellent?

_____

_____

10. How do birds cool off on hot days?

    a. They fly higher in the atmosphere, where the air is cooler.

    b. They lay their feathers flat and pant like dogs.

    c. They shed feathers.

    d. They sweat.

11. Birds eat and digest their food quickly because their metabolisms require a lot of energy. True or False? (Circle one.)

12. How does a gizzard help a bird digest food?

_____

_____

_____

_____

_____

Up, Up, and Away (p. 384)

Choose the bird characteristic in Column B that best matches the use in Column A, and write the corresponding letter in the space provided.

Column A	Column B
_____ **13.** ensuring flight muscles get as much oxygen as possible	**a.** keen eyesight
_____ **14.** maneuvering rapidly	**b.** air sac
_____ **15.** finding food from a distance	**c.** short wing
_____ **16.** soaring	**d.** rigid skeleton
_____ **17.** increasing the bird's oxygen intake	**e.** rapid heart rate
_____ **18.** moving wings powerfully and efficiently	**f.** long, narrow wing

Getting off the Ground (p. 386)

19. The upward pressure on the wing that keeps a bird in the air is

called _____ .

Mark each of the following statements *True* or *False*.

20. _____ The top of a bird's wing is curved so air flowing under the wing moves faster than the air flowing over the wing.

21. _____ The larger the wings, the greater the lift.

22. _____ Birds must flap their wings constantly to stay in the air.

Fly Away (p. 387)

23. Why are the Canada geese in Figure 8 migrating for the winter?

_____

_____

_____

Bringing Up Baby (p. 387)

24. Which of the following is NOT true about brooding?

   a. It keeps a bird's eggs warm.
   b. All birds share the responsibility between males and females.
   c. A bird does this until its eggs hatch.
   d. Birds sit on their eggs.

25. How do cuckoos and cowbirds make other birds work for them?

_____

_____

_____

26. Precocial chicks depend on their parents to feed and protect

them. True or False? (Circle one.)

27. Altricial chicks hatch with their eyes closed. True or False? (Circle one.)

Review (p. 388)

Now that you've finished the first part of Section 1, review what you learned by answering the Review questions in your ScienceLog.

Kinds of Birds (p. 389)

28. One of the smallest birds is the 1.6 g

bee _____ .

29. Look at the description of Flightless Birds on page 389. Describe an adaptation that helps each of the following flightless birds get around.

    a. Ostriches _____

    _____

    b. Penguins _____

    _____

30. Look at the description of Water Birds on page 390. Water birds,

also known as _____ , usually have

_____ feet.

31. What is the the blue-footed booby known for?
    a. remaining underwater for long periods of time
    b. attracting females with beautiful plumage
    c. courting females by raising one foot at a time

32. Look at the description of Birds of Prey at the bottom of page 390. Which of the following is NOT helpful to birds of prey?
    a. keen vision   **c.** strong muscles
    b. sharp claws and beaks   **d.** webbed feet

33. Birds of prey, such as eagles falcons, and hawks, eat meat and

hunt during the _____ .

34. Look at the description of Perching Birds on page 391. Why don't perching birds fall off their perches when they fall asleep?

_____

_____

35. Chickadees sometimes hunt while dangling upside down.

True or False? (Circle one.)

Review (p. 391)

Now that you've finished Section 1, review what you learned by answering the Review questions in your ScienceLog.

Chapter 16, continued

Section 2: Mammals (p. 392)

1. There are more species of _____ than there

   are species of _____ .
   (mollusks or mammals, mollusks or mammals)

2. The largest animal that has ever lived is a mammal. True or False?
   (Circle one.)

The Origin of Mammals (p. 392)

3. Many scientists believe mammals are descended from reptiles

   called _____ .

4. Which of the following statements is NOT true about the first
   mammals?

   a. They appear in the fossil record about 200 million years ago.
   b. They foraged for food at night.
   c. They existed only after dinosaurs became extinct.
   d. They were endotherms.

Characteristics of Mammals (p. 393)

5. Mammary glands are special organs that only female mammals

   have. True or False? (Circle one.)

6. The milk of mammals is made up of fat, water,

   _____ , and _____ .

7. A mammal's body temperature never changes, even when

   hibernating. True or False? (Circle one.)

8. Name two adaptations that help keep mammals warm.

   _____

   _____

   _____

Match the type of tooth in Column B to its use in Column A, and
write the corresponding letter in the space provided.

Column A	Column B
_____ **9.** cutting	**a.** canine
_____ **10.** grinding	**b.** incisor
_____ **11.** stabbing	**c.** molar

12. The shape of a mammal's teeth reflects the

_____ of the mammal. (size or diet)

13. Mammals have _____ sets of teeth.

14. The main purpose of the diaphragm muscle is to

    a. bring air into the lungs.

    b. separate blood with oxygen from blood without oxygen.

    c. provide as much oxygen as possible to the heart.

    d. help mammals make sounds necessary for communication.

15. Mammals use their well-developed senses and large brains to

respond quickly to their environment. True or False?
(Circle one.)

16. Which of the following statements are true of young mammals?
(Circle all that apply.)

    a. They result from sexual reproduction.

    b. They are protected by their parent(s).

    c. They require a lot of care.

    d. They nurse.

Review (p. 395)

Now that you've finished the first part of Section 2, review what you
learned by answering the Review questions in your ScienceLog.

Kinds of Mammals (p. 396)

17. Why are monotremes considered mammals even though they lay
eggs?

_____

_____

_____

18. The duckbilled platypus and the _____
are the only living species of monotremes. Monotremes are

found only in Australia and _____ .

19. A baby platypus gets milk from its mother by licking the milk

from the skin and hair around its mother's nipples. True or False?
(Circle one.)

20. Marsupials lay eggs just like monotremes do. True or False?
(Circle one.)

21. Marsupials use their pouches for

    a. storing food in the winter.
    b. giving birth to their young.
    c. carrying and protecting young.
    d. digesting food for their young.

22. The _____ is the only marsupial living in North America north of Mexico.

23. Female placental mammals do NOT

    a. have a uterus.
    b. supply food and oxygen to their embryo through a placenta.
    c. have a gestation period lasting from a few weeks to many months.
    d. lay eggs

Kinds of Placental Mammals (p. 398)

24. Look at the description of Toothless Mammals on page 398. All toothless mammals, such as armadillos, pangolins, and sloths, have no teeth. True or False? (Circle one.)

25. Most toothless mammals catch insects with a long, sticky tongue. True or False? (Circle one.)

26. Look at the description of Insect Eaters on page 399. Insectivores are tiny mammals that live on every continent except

_____ . Most of them dig in the soil with

their long, pointed _____ .

27. Look at the description of Rodents on page 399. Rodents gnaw so much that they grow several sets of teeth. True or False? (Circle one.)

28. Look at the description of Lagomorphs on page 400. Which of the following is NOT a characteristic of a lagomorph?

    a. sensitive nose   **c.** two sets of incisors
    b. large ears   **d.** long tail

29. Look at the description of Flying Mammals on page 400. Explain how bats use sound to find their dinner.

_____

_____

_____

_____

30. Look at page 401. Animals that eat almost only meat are called

_____ . Meat-eaters have large canines

and special _____ for slicing meat.

31. Some carnivores eat _____ as well as meat.

32. Look at page 402. Hoofed mammals are divided into groups

based on the thickness of their hooves. True or False?
(Circle one.)

33. Giraffes are the tallest living mammals. True or False?
(Circle one.)

34. Look at page 403. Elephants use their trunk the same

way we use our nose, _____ , and

_____ .

35. Look at the description of Cetaceans on page 404. Sperm whales
are cetaceans that use echolocation to stun their food as well as
to find it. True or False? (Circle one.)

36. Look at the description of Sirenia on page 404. Which of the
following characteristics does NOT describe sirenia, such as man-
atees or dugongs?

    a. plant-eaters

    b. completely aquatic

    c. quiet

    d. make up the largest group of mammals

Look at the description of Primates on page 405. Mark each of the
following statements *True* or *False.*

37. _____ Monkeys, humans, and prosimians are all primates.

38. _____ Primates have large brains in proportion to their
body size.

39. _____ In primates, the eyes face forward.

40. _____ All primates have five fingers on each hand and
five toes on each foot.

41. _____ All primates live on the ground.

42. _____ Primates have claws.

Review (p. 405)

Now that you've finished Section 2, review what you learned by
answering the Review questions in your ScienceLog.

CHAPTER

17 DIRECTED READING WORKSHEET

The Earth's Ecosystems

As you read Chapter 17, which begins on page 414 of your textbook, answer the following questions.

Would You Believe . . . ? (p. 414)

1. How does the Venus' flytrap get nutrients?

_____

_____

2. How does the Venus' flytrap relate to the subject matter in this chapter?

   a. The Venus' flytrap is well adapted to its environment.

   b. The Venus' flytrap is a carnivore, and the chapter discusses nutrition.

   c. The Venus' flytrap is the only plant that does not photosynthesize.

   d. The Venus' flytrap cannot be hurt by humans.

What Do You Think? (p. 415)

Answer these questions in your ScienceLog now. Then later, you'll have a chance to revise your answers based on what you've learned.

Investigate! (p. 415)

3. What is the purpose of this activity?

_____

_____

_____

_____

Section 1: Land Ecosystems (p. 416)

4. _____ factors are features of an environment that are not alive, such as temperature and rainfall.

The Earth's Biomes (p. 416)

Mark each of the following statements *True* or *False*.

5. _____ A biome is an area characterized by abiotic factors.

6. _____ A biome is made up of many ecosystems.

7. _____ A particular type of biome can exist in only one place on Earth.

8. How many different biomes are shown in Figure 1?

　　a. 7　　　　　　　　　**c.** 9
　　b. 8　　　　　　　　　**d.** 10

Forests (p. 417)

9. Name the three main types of forest biomes.

_____

_____

10. The term *deciduous* originates from a Latin word that means

　　a. "to change color."　　**c.** "to decide."
　　b. "to fall off."　　　　**d.** "to change seasons."

11. Coniferous forests are characterized mainly by trees that don't lose their leaves and stay green during the winter.

　　True or False? (Circle one.)

12. A _____ _____ on the leaves or needles of conifers protects the leaves from drying out during the winter.

13. There is little vegetation on the floor of a coniferous forest partly because

　　a. there are not enough nutrients in the soil.
　　b. the roots of coniferous trees produce a chemical that prohibits such growth.
　　c. little light reaches the forest floor.
　　d. the vegetation cannot survive the harsh winters.

14. In a tropical rain forest, how many species of trees can live in an area one-fourth the size of a football field?

_____

Chapter 17, continued

15. Where do most animals live in the rain forest?

    a. on the ground   **c.** in the canopy

    b. in low-lying vines   **d.** None of the above

16. A tropical rain forest biome has most of its nutrients in its

    _____ . (soil or vegetation)

Grasslands (p. 420)

17. Savannas, pampas, steppes, plains, and prairies are all examples of grasslands. True or False? (Circle one.)

18. _____ prevent many trees from growing in the grasslands.

Mark each of the following statements *True* or *False*.

19. _____ There are no flowering plants in grasslands.

20. _____ A savanna contains scattered clumps of trees.

21. _____ Giraffes, elephants, and zebras can be found in African savannas.

Deserts (p. 421)

22. How are different plants adapted to living in the desert?

    _____

    _____

    _____

    _____

    _____

    _____

23. Name a desert animal. Then explain how one adaption of the animal helps it live in the desert.

    _____

    _____

    _____

    _____

    _____

▲▲ CHAPTER 17
▲▲
▲

24. Do you live in a desert biome? Justify your answer.

_____

_____

_____

_____

_____

_____

_____

_____

Tundra (p. 422)

25. Permafrost thaws out for only 2 months of the year.

True or False? (Circle one.)

26. Considering there is very little rainfall in the tundra, why is water plentiful?

_____

_____

_____

_____

_____

27. The _____ tundra gets a lot of sunlight.

28. Which of the biomes discussed in this section gets the most average yearly rainfall?

_____

29. Which of the biomes discussed in this section gets the least average yearly rainfall?

_____

Review (p. 422)

Now that you've finished Section 1, review what you learned by answering the Review questions in your ScienceLog.

Chapter 17, continued

Section 2: Marine Ecosystems (p. 423)

1. The Earth's oceans and seas contain about half of the Earth's water supply. True or False? (Circle one.)

2. A marine ecosystem contains

    a. acidic water.   **c.** sour water.

    b. salty water.   **d.** bitter water.

Abiotic Factors Rule (p. 423)

3. Which of the following abiotic factors determine what different areas of the ocean are like? (Circle all that apply.)

    a. the temperature

    b. the amount of sunlight penetrating the water

    c. the distance from land

    d. the depth of the water

4. Producers are found only to a depth of about

_____ m below the ocean's surface.

5. How are phytoplankton and zooplankton different?

_____

_____

_____

_____

Wonderful Watery Biomes (p. 424)

6. Suppose you could walk into an ocean and swim to the center of it, in what order would you pass through the following zones? Write the appropriate number in the space provided.

_____ intertidal

_____ oceanic

_____ neritic

_____ benthic

7. In which zone of an ocean do you find the most-unusual animals? Explain.

_____

_____

_____

CHAPTER 17

Chapter 17, continued

A Closer Look (p. 426)

8. Which of the following are ways that marine environments affect us? (Circle all that apply.)

    a. They provide most of the water for rainfall on our planet.
    b. They supply us with food.
    c. Their temperatures affect climates and wind patterns.
    d. None of the above

9. Explain the symbiotic relationship between corals and algae.

_____

_____

_____

_____

10. In the _____ most of the animals have adapted to living with huge floating rafts of algae.

11. The ocean water around Antarctica is rich in nutrients. Where did these nutrients come from?

_____

_____

12. Most life in the Arctic Ocean feeds off the large aquatic mammals. True or False? (Circle one.)

13. An estuary is a special type of river. True or False? (Circle one.)

14. The rise and fall of the tide affects the amount of

_____ in an estuary.

15. How do sea anemones avoid being washed out to sea?

_____

_____

Review (p. 427)

Now that you've finished Section 2, review what you learned by answering the Review questions in your ScienceLog.

Section 3: Freshwater Ecosystems (p. 428)

1. One of the most important characteristics of freshwater

    ecosystems is the _____ the water is
    moving.

Water on the Move (p. 428)

2. How have producers adapted to living in moving freshwater?

    a. They do not need as much sunlight.
    b. They can float.
    c. They are strong and can withstand wave action.
    d. They cling to rocks.

3. Some consumers that live in moving water have adapted to their

    environment by using suction _____ to
    hold onto rocks. (disks or cups)

4. All moving water eventually empties into a lake or an ocean.

    True or False? (Circle one.)

Still Waters (p. 429)

5. The largest lake in the world is Lake _____ .

6. The most abundant producers in the open-water littoral zone of
    a lake are

    a. bacteria.   **c.** phytoplankton.
    b. long-leafed plants.   **d.** carp.

7. What determines the depth of the open-water zone?

    _____

    _____

8. Deep-water-zone organisms must hunt their food.

    True or False? (Circle one)

Wetlands (p. 430)

9. Which of the following is NOT true about wetlands?

    a. For most of the year, the water level is above or near the
    ground.
    b. They are important in flood control.
    c. They replenish underground water supplies.
    d. They support very few species of plant and animal life.

10. Freshwater marshes occur beside rivers and oceans. True or False?
    (Circle one.)

CHAPTER 17

11. A _____ has trees but a
_____ does not.
(swamp or marsh, swamp or marsh)

12. How have trees adapted to living in a swamp?

_____

_____

_____

_____

From Lake to Forest (p. 431)

13. How can a pond or a lake become a forest?

_____

_____

_____

_____

_____

14. The three types of ecosystems you learned about in this chapter are
  a. ground, maritime, and fresh.
  b. land, ocean, and stream.
  c. land, marine, and freshwater.

Review (p. 431)

Now that you've finished Section 3, review what you learned by
answering the Review questions in your ScienceLog.

CHAPTER

18 **DIRECTED READING WORKSHEET**

Environmental Problems and Solutions

As you read Chapter 18, which begins on page 438 of your textbook, answer the following questions.

Imagine . . . (p. 438)

1. Linen and cotton rags were used by the American colonists to

   make paper. True or False? (Circle one.)

2. Pulp from trees is the main ingredient in most of the paper we use today. What is the main ingredient in Haifa Aldorasi's homemade paper?

   _____

   _____

What Do You Think? (p. 439)

Answer these questions in your ScienceLog now. Then later, you'll have a chance to revise your answers based on what you've learned.

Investigate! (p. 439)

3. How do you think the optional ingredients (flower petals, orange peel, etc.) might affect the finished product?

   _____

   _____

Section 1: First the Bad News (p. 440)

4. What is the bad news about our planet, Earth?

   _____

   _____

   _____

Pollution (p. 440)

5. All of the following can be pollutants EXCEPT

   a. chemicals.   **c.** noise.

   b. water.   **d.** heat.

6. How much trash does the average American throw away in a week?

   a. 1 kg   **c.** 12 kg

   b. 2 kg   **d.** 14 kg

▲ ▲ ▲ **CHAPTER 18**

7. Waste that is harmful to _____ and the environment is hazardous waste.

8. Name three hazardous wastes you might have in your home.

_____

_____

_____

9. It is always illegal to bury hazardous wastes.

True or False? (Circle one.)

10. How do individuals and industries get rid of trash? (Circle all that apply.)

a. They take it to landfills.
b. They dump it into rivers.
c. They bury it.
d. They burn it.

11. Look at Figure 3. When and how did most people first become aware of the dangers of pesticides?

_____

_____

_____

Mark each of the following statements *True* or *False*.

12. _____ The destruction of the layer of ozone that protects the Earth from ultraviolet light is caused by CFCs.

13. _____ Today, CFCs are commonly used in refrigerators and plastics.

14. _____ PCBs are poisonous.

15. _____ The use of PCBs is now banned.

16. _____ In the environment, PCBs break down rapidly.

17. Which of the following can exposure to radioactive wastes cause in humans? (Circle all that apply.)

a. sickle cell anemia **c.** leukemia
b. cancer **d.** birth defects

18. It only takes 100 years for radioactive wastes to become harmless.

True or False? (Circle one.)

19. Place the following events related to global temperature in the correct order. Write the appropriate number in the space provided.

_____ flooding of coastal areas

_____ increase in global temperatures

_____ increased levels of carbon dioxide in the atmosphere

_____ melting of polar icecaps

20. What are the possible negative effects of noise pollution?

_____

_____

_____

21. Look at the Earth Science Connection on page 442. Which of the following can be caused by increased levels of ultraviolet light? (Circle all that apply)

   a. skin cancer   **c.** a weakened immune system

   b. lower crop yields   **d.** blindness

Review (p. 442)

Now that you've finished the first part of Section 1, review what you learned by answering the Review questions in your ScienceLog.

Resource Depletion (p. 443)

Identify each of the following resources as renewable or nonrenewable. Write *R* if it is renewable, and *NR* if it is nonrenewable.

22. _____ fresh water

23. _____ fossil fuels

24. _____ oil

25. _____ solar energy

26. _____ many minerals

27. The damage shown in Figure 6 was caused by a method of mining called _____ mining.

28. Why are some renewable resources like underground water and soil becoming nonrenewable?

   a. Underground water and soil form quickly.

   b. People are using them up faster than they can be replaced.

   c. There has been an increase in biodiversity.

   d. These resources are not naturally renewable, as was previously thought.

Chapter 18, continued

Alien Species (p. 444)

29. How do humans help spread organisms around the world?

_____

_____

_____

30. Alien species are organisms that aren't native to a geographical

area. True or False? (Circle one.)

31. Give an example of how an alien species can cause damage to
the environment.

_____

_____

_____

_____

Human Population Growth (p. 444)

32. Some people think that there are too many people on the Earth
today because there are many people who don't have enough

food to eat. True or False? (Circle one.)

33. Do you think the Earth will be able to support 14 billion people
in the year 2100? Why or why not?

_____

_____

_____

_____

Habitat Destruction (p. 445)

34. "_____ of life" is the meaning of the word
biodiversity.

35. If a habitat is destroyed,
   a. certain plant species always become extinct.
   b. certain animal species always become extinct.
   c. the plants and animals will flourish elsewhere.
   d. biodiversity is lost.

36. Trees once covered three times as much land as they do today.

True or False? (Circle one.)

37. Because tropical soil has few _____ , little can grow on the land after tropical rain forests have been cleared.

38. Why is the preservation of wetlands important to humans? (Circle all that apply.)

   a. Wetlands help control flooding.
   b. Wetlands help prevent soil erosion.
   c. Wetlands are a source of land for new construction sites.
   d. Wetlands filter pollutants from flowing water.

39. One of the primary contributors to the loss of marine habitats is

_____ .

40. Plastics are harmful to animals and the environment because

they are not _____ .

Effects on Humans (p. 446)

41. Pollution that occurred 30 years ago can affect your health today.

True or False? (Circle one.)

Review (p. 446)

Now that you've finished Section 1, review what you learned by answering the Review questions in your ScienceLog.

Section 2: The Good News: Solutions (p. 447)

1. This section is about what _____ can do to save the Earth.

Conservation (p. 447)

2. What is one thing you can do to conserve natural resources that isn't mentioned in your text?

_____

_____

_____

_____

_____

Chapter 18, continued

3. The three R's of conservation stand for _____ ,

_____ and _____ .

4. Look at Figure 13. How do you think using a cloth shopping bag reduces the need for natural resources?

_____

_____

_____

_____

Reduce (p. 448)

5. How much of the waste produced in cities is from packaging?

   a. one-half   **c.** one-fourth
   b. one-third   **d.** two-thirds

6. Organic farmers do not use _____ and

_____ fertilizers.

7. Which of the following is NOT an alternative power source?

   a. falling water
   b. winds
   c. tides
   d. coal

8. Look at Figure 15. How are the people in Rotterdam, Holland, reducing their dependence on fossil fuels?

_____

_____

_____

9. A citizen of the United States produces _____ times more garbage than a citizen of a developing country.

Reuse (p. 449)

10. _____ plants and _____ animals can be used to clean waste water.

11. What can reclaimed waste water be used for?

   a. drinking   **c.** cooking
   b. watering lawns   **d.** making ice cubes

Chapter 18, continued

Recycle (p. 449)

12. What is the difference between recycling and reusing?

_____

_____

_____

13. Using Figure 18 on page 449, list two household items you use that can be recycled.

_____

_____

_____

14. Half a million trees are used to print Sunday newspapers every week. True or False? (Circle one.)

15. Resource recovery is the process of

    a. transforming garbage into nuclear power.
    b. transforming garbage into electricity.
    c. water reclamation.
    d. recycling bottles and cans.

16. The United States recycles only about

_____ percent of the garbage it generates.

Review (p. 450)

Now that you've finished the first part of Section 2, review what you learned by answering the Review questions in your ScienceLog.

Maintaining Biodiversity (p. 451)

17. Biodiversity

    a. helps to keep communities stable.
    b. occurs when a geographic area contains only one species.
    c. is shown in Figure 21.
    d. has no effect on the environment.

18. Individual species are protected by the Endangered Species Act.

True or False? (Circle one.)

19. The Endangered Species Act does not require the development of programs that help endangered species recover.

True or False? (Circle one.)

CHAPTER 18

20. Why are places like the nature preserve shown in Figure 23 important?

_____

_____

_____

_____

Strategies (p. 452)

21. Which of the strategies on page 452 can *you* use to preserve the Earth's habitats?

_____

_____

_____

_____

_____

_____

What *You* Can Do (p. 453)

22. Look at the list on page 453. Give a personal example of a way you have practiced one of those ways of reducing, reusing, or recycling.

_____

_____

_____

_____

Review (p. 453)

Now that you've finished Section 2, review what you've learned by answering the Review questions in your ScienceLog.

CHAPTER

19 DIRECTED READING WORKSHEET

Body Organization and Structure

As you read Chapter 19, which begins on page 462 of your textbook, answer the following questions.

This Really Happened . . . (p. 462)

1. The people who were wearing life jackets didn't drown after the *Titanic* struck an iceberg. Why did they die?

_____

_____

_____

2. In this chapter, you'll learn how our bodies maintain a constant

_____ temperature.

What Do You Think? (p. 463)

Answer these questions in your ScienceLog now. Then later, you'll have a chance to revise your answers based on what you've learned.

Investigate! (p. 463)

3. You experience pain when someone steps on your toe. What is your body trying to tell you?

_____

_____

Section 1: Body Organization (p. 464)

4. How did Jack Thayer survive in the icy water during the *Titanic* disaster?

_____

_____

_____

5. Homeostasis is the maintenance of a

_____ _____

environment.

6. Cells can die if homeostasis is disrupted. True or False? (Circle one.)

▲ ▲ **CHAPTER 19**
▲

Four Types of Tissue (p. 464)

7. How is your body like a soccer team?

_____

_____

_____

_____

Look at Figure 1 on pages 464–465. Then match each tissue type in Column B with its correct function in Column A, and write the corresponding letter in the space provided.

Column A	Column B
____ **8.** joins, supports, and insulates organs	**a.** nervous tissue
____ **9.** covers and protects underlying tissue	**b.** muscle tissue
____ **10.** sends electrical signals through the body	**c.** epithelial tissue
____ **11.** produces movement	**d.** connective tissue

Tissues Form Organs (p. 465)

12. Several types of tissue working together can do jobs that one

type of tissue could not do by itself. True or False? (Circle one.)

Use Figure 2 to answer questions 13–15.

13. How does your brain know when your stomach is full?

_____

_____

_____

14. Muscle tissue helps your stomach digest food by

   a. protecting the stomach during digestion.
   b. supplying the stomach with oxygen.
   c. crushing and grinding stomach contents.
   d. producing the acids that are used during digestion.

15. The stomach is supplied with _____ by the blood.

16. The inside of your stomach is lined with

_____ tissue.

Organs Form Systems (p. 465)

17. Your stomach does all the work of digesting your food.

   True or False? (Circle one.)

Use the diagrams of human organ systems on pages 466–467 to answer the following questions. Each of the following statements is false. Change the underlined word to make the statement true. Write the new word in the space provided.

18. The <u>digestive</u> system provides a frame to protect and support body parts.

   _____

19. Your cardiovascular system consists of your heart and blood vessels, which <u>break down</u> blood throughout your body.

   _____

20. The <u>nervous</u> system releases chemical messengers from certain glands that regulate body functions.

   _____

21. In your respiratory system, your lungs absorb <u>nutrients</u> and release carbon dioxide.

   _____

22. Your <u>integumentary</u> system returns leaked fluids to your blood vessels and helps you get rid of harmful germs.

   _____

23. Your <u>skeletal</u> system allows you to move your bones.

   _____

24. The male reproductive system produces and delivers <u>eggs</u>.

   _____

25. The urinary system removes wastes from the blood and regulates the body's <u>temperature</u>.

   _____

Review (p. 467)

Now that you've finished Section 1, review what you learned by answering the Review questions in your ScienceLog.

Section 2: The Skeletal System (p. 468)

1. Your skeleton is alive. True or False? (Circle one.)

The Burden of Being a Bone (p. 468)

2. Look at Figure 3. Which of the following statements are true about human bones? (Circle all that apply.)

   a. Some bones contain a material that makes white blood cells.
   b. Arm bones have hollow cavities that store fat.
   c. Bones protect your brain, heart, lungs, and spinal cord.
   d. Without bones, you could still sit.
   e. Adult humans have 260 bones.
   f. Bones store minerals.

What's in a Bone? (p. 469)

3. Bones contain two different kinds of bone tissue.

   True or False? (Circle one.)

Determine whether each of the following statements is true of compact bone or spongy bone. In the space provided, write a *C* if it is true of compact bone and an *S* if it is true of spongy bone.

4. _____ It has many open spaces.

5. _____ It is where red blood cells are made.

6. _____ It contains small blood vessels.

7. _____ It contains tiny canals.

8. _____ It contains marrow.

9. _____ It provides most of the strength for the bone.

Growing Bones (p. 470)

10. Most of your skeleton was soft and rubbery when you were born.

    True or False? (Circle one.)

11. How do bones continue to grow during childhood?

    _____

    _____

    _____

12. In Figure 5, the cartilage does not show up on the X ray because

    cartilage does not have the _____ density
    of bone.

Chapter 19, continued

What's the Point of a Joint? (p. 470)

Use the text and Figure 6 to match the term in Column B with the correct phrase in Column A, and write the corresponding letter in the space provided.

Column A	Column B
____ **13.** immovable joint found in the skull	**a.** sliding joint
____ **14.** allows motion in all directions	**b.** ligament
____ **15.** allows you to only flex and extend	**c.** fixed joint
____ **16.** cushion found where two bones meet	**d.** joint
____ **17.** the place where two or more bones connect	**e.** hinge joint
____ **18.** elastic bands of tissue that hold joints together	**f.** ball-and-socket joint
____ **19.** allows bones to glide over one another	**g.** cartilage

Can Levers Lessen Your Load? (p. 471)

20. Your limbs are examples of simple machines. True or False? (Circle one.)

21. The measure of how many times a simple machine multiplies an

_____ applied to a

_____ is known as the mechanical

advantage.

22. Which of the pictures in Figure 7 shows a lever that cannot increase force?

_____

_____

_____

Review (p. 471)

Now that you've finished Section 2, review what you learned by answering the Review questions in your ScienceLog.

Section 3: The Muscular System (p. 472)

1. Why can't you stay perfectly still no matter how hard you try?

_____

_____

2. The muscular system is made up of

_____ and _____ .

Types of Muscle (p. 472)

Mark each of the following statements *True* or *False*.

3. _____ Cardiac muscle is found only in the heart.

4. _____ When smooth muscle moves blood through your blood vessels, the action is voluntary.

5. _____ The actions of skeletal muscles are always voluntary.

6. _____ Cardiac-muscle action is always involuntary.

7. _____ Skeletal muscles help protect your inner organs.

8. _____ There are three types of muscle: cardiac, voluntary and skeletal.

Making Your Move (p. 473)

9. To make a funny face, what has to happen in your body?

_____

_____

_____

_____

10. Look at Figure 9. It takes more muscles to smile than to frown.

True or False? (Circle one.)

11. Tendons are strands of connective tissue that connect

_____ to _____ .

12. Most skeletal muscles

   a. work independently.
   b. are connected to each other by bones.
   c. are strands of tough connective tissue.
   d. work in pairs.

13. When your arm is extended, the triceps muscle

   a. is bending.   **c.** is the flexor.
   b. acts involuntarily.   **d.** is the extensor.

Chapter 19, continued

Use It or Lose It (p. 474)

14. How does having strong muscles benefit the rest of the body?

_____

_____

_____

_____

_____

_____

15. A resistance exercise requires the _____
to overcome the weight of another object.

16. Aerobic exercises, such as swimming, are best for strengthening

your _____ and for increasing the

_____ of your

_____ muscles.

Muscle Injury (p. 475)

17. List two things that can cause a muscle to overstretch or tear.

_____

_____

_____

18. When tendons are overused, they can become

_____ . (immobile or inflamed)

19. Which of the following characteristics of anabolic steroids is
NOT true?

a. They resemble a male sex hormone.
b. They threaten the heart.
c. They cause immature bones to stop growing.
d. They make muscles bigger and stronger.
e. They make you lose weight.

Review (p. 475)

Now that you've finished Section 3, review what you learned by
answering the Review questions in your ScienceLog.

▲▲ CHAPTER 19

Section 4: The Integumentary System (p. 476)

1. What organ comes in a variety of colors, is partly dead, and protects people from the outside world?

_____

_____

_____

2. The integumentary system is made up of

_____ , _____ ,

and _____ .

The Skin: More than Just a "Coat" (p. 476)

3. Which of the following are true of skin?
(Circle all that apply.)

   a. It contains nerve endings.
   b. It uses sweat to keep you warm.
   c. It keeps moisture inside the body.
   d. It releases sweat that removes wastes from the bloodstream.

4. Darker skin has more melanin than lighter skin. True or False?
(Circle one.)

5. How does the melanin in your skin help prevent cancer?

_____

_____

_____

_____

A Tale of Two Layers (p. 477)

Mark each of the following statements *True* or *False*.

6. _____ The epidermis is thicker than the dermis.

7. _____ Epidermal cells have no known function because they are dead.

8. _____ The dermis is strong yet flexible.

9. _____ Skin is a complex organ that contains many smaller structures.

10. Look at Figure 16. The oil glands in your skin

    a. make oil that causes the hair to stand up straight.

    b. make oil that helps keep the epidermis waterproof.

    c. help the sweat glands make extra sweat.

    d. make oil that keeps the hair hard and brittle.

Hair and Nails (p. 478)

11. All the living cells in your hair are in the hair

    _____ .

12. Hairs do not block ultraviolet light. True or False? (Circle one.)

13. Hair and skin use different pigments for color. True or False? (Circle one.)

14. What causes a goose bump to form?

    _____

    _____

    _____

    _____

    _____

15. A furry animal might get goose bumps on a cold day because

    a. the muscles attached to the hair follicles contract.

    b. the lifted hairs block the wind.

    c. the animal looks bigger.

    d. making "goose bumps" uses a lot of energy and takes extra heat.

16. Your nails decrease the sensitivity of your fingertips.

    True or False? (Circle one.)

Living in Harm's Way (p. 479)

17. Look at Figure 19. How does your skin heal itself when you get a cut?

    _____

    _____

    _____

    _____

CHAPTER 19

18. Look at Figure 20. What is the difference between an ordinary mole and a mole that may become cancerous?

    a. Cancerous moles are darker than ordinary moles.

    b. Cancerous moles are more symmetrical than ordinary moles.

    c. Cancerous moles are smaller than ordinary moles.

    d. Cancerous moles are more asymmetrical than ordinary moles.

Answer the following questions after you finish reading page 479. Match each term in Column B with the correct phrase in Column A, and write the corresponding letter in the space provided.

Column A	Column B
_____ **19.** caused by hair follicles clogged with oil, dead skin cells, and bacteria	**a.** skin
_____ **20.** a mass of skin cells caused by uncontrolled cell division	**b.** mole
_____ **21.** darkened area of the skin	**c.** cancer
_____ **22.** the most exposed part of the body	**d.** sex hormones
_____ **23.** a tumor that invades other tissues	**e.** infections
_____ **24.** chemicals that cause oil glands to produce too much oil	**f.** tumor

Review (p. 479)

Now that you've finished Section 4, review what you learned by answering the Review questions in your Science Log.

CHAPTER

20 DIRECTED READING WORKSHEET

Circulation and Respiration

As you read Chapter 20, which begins on page 486 of your textbook, answer the following questions.

This Really Happened . . . (p. 486)

1. What can doctors do if a person's heart fails?

_____

_____

_____

2. In this chapter, you will study all of the following systems EXCEPT

    a. the respiratory system.   **c.** the cardiovascular system.

    b. the digestive system.   **d.** the lymphatic system.

What Do You Think? (p. 487)

Answer these questions in your ScienceLog now. Then later, you'll have a chance to revise your answers based on what you've learned.

Investigate! (p. 487)

3. What causes the throbbing called a pulse?

_____

_____

_____

Section 1: The Cardiovascular System (p. 488)

4. The system that transports materials to and from your

_____ is made up of blood, the

_____ , and blood

_____ .

What Is Blood? (p. 488)

5. Your blood is a type of connective tissue.

    True or False? (Circle one.)

CHAPTER 20

6. Which of the following make up the plasma?
(Circle all that apply.)

a. red blood cells
b. water
c. proteins
d. platelets
e. minerals
f. white blood cells
g. nutrients
h. sugars

7. How does the shape of a red blood cell make it especially well suited for its job?

_____

_____

_____

Mark each of the following statements *True* or *False*.

8. _____ Hemoglobin is a cell that helps to transport the oxygen you inhale to the rest of your body.

9. _____ The bone marrow is where red blood cells are produced.

10. _____ Red blood cells have a relatively short life span because they have no DNA and cannot make proteins.

Answer questions 11–15 after you finish reading about white blood cells on page 489. Choose the term in Column B that best matches the phrase in Column A, and write the corresponding letter in the space provided.

Column A	Column B
___ **11.** a tiny particle that can make you sick	**a.** antibody
___ **12.** a chemical that some WBCs release to help fight intruders	**b.** pathogen
___ **13.** formed in the bone marrow	**c.** white blood cell
___ **14.** where some WBCs mature	**d.** lymphatic organ

15. Which of the following statements are true of platelets?
(Circle all that apply.)

a. They last for 5 to 10 days.
b. They pinch off fragments of themselves to form a blood clot.
c. They are fragments of larger cells.
d. They help reduce blood loss.

Chapter 20, continued

Have a Heart (p. 490)

16. Your heart is a four-chambered muscular organ about the size of your

    a. stomach.   **c.** liver.

    b. nose.   **d.** fist.

17. What causes the lub-dub sounds of your heartbeat?

_____

_____

_____

Use the diagram on page 490 to place the following steps of blood flow through the heart in the correct order. Write the appropriate number in the space provided.

18. _____ Blood is squeezed into the ventricles when the atria contract.

19. _____ Blood enters the atria.

20. _____ Blood is pushed out of the heart when the atria relax and the ventricles contract.

Blood Vessels (p. 491)

21. Look at Figure 8. Capillaries connect

_____ to

_____ .

(large veins or small veins, large arteries or small arteries)

Choose the type of blood vessel in Column B that best matches the description in Column A, and write the corresponding letter in the space provided. Blood vessels can be used more than once.

Column A	Column B
_____ **22.** smallest blood vessels in the body	**a.** arteries
_____ **23.** direct blood away from the heart	**b.** capillaries
_____ **24.** many substances can diffuse through their walls	**c.** veins
_____ **25.** direct blood back to the heart	
_____ **26.** push blood with the help of skeletal muscles	
_____ **27.** very close to all living cells in the body	
_____ **28.** have thick walls to withstand pressure	

CHAPTER 20

Going with the Flow (p. 492)

29. Pulmonary circulation is the process during which blood obtains oxygen from the lungs. True or False? (Circle one.)

30. Systemic circulation is the circulation of blood between the heart and the lungs. True or False? (Circle one.)

Use the diagram on page 492 to answer the following questions. Indicate whether each of the following statements is a part of pulmonary or systemic circulation. In the space provided, write *P* if it is part of pulmonary circulation and *S* if it is part of systemic circulation.

31. _____ Oxygen-poor blood travels through arteries to the lungs.

32. _____ Oxygen-poor blood is delivered to the right atrium of the heart by two large veins.

33. _____ The blood releases carbon dioxide and absorbs oxygen.

34. _____ Oxygen, nutrients, and water are delivered to the body's cells.

35. _____ Oxygen-rich blood pumps from the left ventricle into arteries.

Blood Flows Under Pressure (p. 493)

36. How is blood running through your veins like water running through a hose?

_____

_____

_____

_____

_____

37. The units that blood pressure is reported in are _____ .

38. Figure 10 shows a person getting his blood pressure checked. How might your blood pressure indicate a problem with your cardiovascular system?

_____

_____

_____

_____

Chapter 20, continued

39. In a normal blood pressure reading of 120/80, the number 80 stands for the pressure in the

    a. arteries when the ventricles relax.

    b. arteries when the ventricles contract.

    c. ventricles when the ventricles relax.

    d. ventricles when the ventricles contract.

Exercise and Blood Flow (p. 493)

Mark each of the following statements *True* or *False*.

40. _____ When you exercise, blood flow is reduced to the brain, heart, and lungs so that more blood can go to the muscles.

41. _____ Some of your organs, like your kidneys, do not need oxygen when you exercise.

42. _____ When your heart beats faster, more oxygen and nutrients are being delivered to your muscles.

43. _____ When all the "water faucets" in the body are open, the heart rate slows down.

44. _____ Your brain directs blood flow.

Review (p. 493)

Now that you've finished reading the first part of Section 1, review what you've learned by answering the Review questions in your ScienceLog.

What's Your Blood Type? (p. 494)

45. Is it safe to give a person blood of any type? Explain.

_____

_____

_____

_____

_____

46. Everyone has type _____ , _____ , _____ , or _____ blood.

Each of the following statements is false. Change the underlined word to make the statement true. Write the new word in the space provided.

47. Blood type is determined by the <u>antibodies</u> present on the surface of your red blood cells.

_____

48. <u>Type O</u> blood has both A and B antigens.

_____

49. Certain chemicals in plasma, called <u>enzymes</u>, can bind to RBCs and cause the RBCs to clump together.

_____

50. Type O people are universal <u>recipients</u>.

_____

Cardiovascular Problems (p. 495)

51. Cardiovascular problems occur only in the heart. True or False? (Circle one.)

52. Cardiovascular problems affect the movement of _____ through the body.

53. What is wrong with the blood vessel shown in Figure 12?

_____

_____

_____

_____

54. Which of the following statements is NOT true about hypertension?

    a. It is promoted by atherosclerosis.
    b. It weakens blood vessels.
    c. It is an abnormally low blood pressure.
    d. It can lead to a stroke.

55. List three things mentioned in the text that people can do to reduce their risk of cardiovascular disease.

_____

_____

_____

_____

Review (p. 495)

Now that you've finished Section 1, review what you learned by answering the Review questions in your ScienceLog.

Section 2: The Lymphatic System (p. 496)

1. Your cells are bathed in fluid. What happens to that fluid?

_____

_____

_____

2. The lymphatic system and the cardiovascular system are both

_____ systems.

Vessels of the Lymphatic System (p. 496)

3. Besides fluid, the lymph also contains

_____ that are too large to enter the blood capillaries.

4. Lymph is carried into lymphatic vessels by

_____ , the smallest vessels of the lymphatic system.

5. Lymph is not pushed through the lymphatic system by a pump. How does it move?

_____

_____

_____

Lymphatic Organs (p. 497)

Answer questions 6–10 after you finish reading page 497. Match the terms in Column B with the correct phrase in Column A, and write the corresponding letter in the space provided.

Column A	Column B
____ **6.** white blood cells that mark pathogens for destruction	**a.** lymph nodes
____ **7.** small organs that remove pathogens and dead cells from the lymph	**b.** thymus
____ **8.** recycling center for red blood cells	**c.** lymphocytes
____ **9.** organ above your heart which releases WBCs	**d.** tonsils
____ **10.** structures inside your throat that help defend against infection	**e.** spleen

Review (p. 497)

Now that you've finished Section 2, review what you learned by answering the Review questions in your ScienceLog.

Section 3: The Respiratory System (p. 498)

1. Most of the time, you don't think about breathing. When might you think about breathing?

_____

_____

_____

Out with the Bad Air; In with the Good (p. 498)

2. You breathe to absorb carbon dioxide from the air.

True or False? (Circle one.)

3. Your body adds carbon dioxide to the air you exhale.

True or False? (Circle one.)

4. Which of the following statements are true about respiration? (Circle all that apply.)

   a. It is the same thing as breathing.
   b. It includes breathing.
   c. It includes cellular respiration.
   d. It includes the process by which your body absorbs water.

Chapter 20, continued

Breathing: Brought to You by Your Respiratory System (p. 498)

Use the text on pages 498–499 and Figure 15 to put the following steps of air flow into your lungs in the correct order. Write the appropriate number in the space provided.

5. _____ Air flows into one of two tubes and then goes into the lungs.

6. _____ Air flows past the vocal cords.

7. _____ Air flows through a tube that sometimes contains food and water.

8. _____ Air flows through the windpipe.

9. _____ Air is inhaled through the primary passageway of the respiratory system.

10. _____ Air flows into thousands of tiny sacs inside the lungs.

11. Look at the Earth Science Connection. Why do people who live at low elevations have trouble exerting themselves when they travel to the mountains?

_____

_____

_____

_____

_____

How Do You Breathe? (p. 500)

12. Your lungs don't contain any muscle. So how is air sucked into your lungs?

_____

_____

_____

_____

13. Cellular respiration is a chemical reaction that occurs when

_____ is used to release

_____ stored in molecules of carbohydrates, fats, and proteins. Carbon dioxide and

_____ are also released.

CHAPTER 20

Chapter 20, continued

Respiratory Disorders (p. 501)

Match each disease in Column B with the correct description in
Column A, and write the corresponding letter in the space provided.

Column A	Column B
_____ **14.** caused by bacteria or viruses that grow in the bronchioles and alveoli	**a.** lung cancer
_____ **15.** can occur when chemicals in tobacco smoke cause lung cells to form tumors	**b.** asthma
_____ **16.** involves an increase in mucus secretion and narrowing of the bronchioles	**c.** emphysema
_____ **17.** can develop when something irritates the bronchiole lining	**d.** pneumonia
_____ **18.** occurs when alveoli erode away	**e.** bronchitis

19. How can a tumor in your lung endanger the rest of your body?

_____

_____

_____

_____

_____

_____

Review (p. 501)

Now that you've finished Section 3, review what you learned by
answering the Review questions in your ScienceLog.

CHAPTER

21 **DIRECTED READING WORKSHEET**

Communication and Control

As you read Chapter 21, which begins on page 508 of your textbook, answer the following questions.

This Really Happened . . . ! (p. 508)

1. How did the rod going through Phineas Gage's head change the way scientists view the brain?

_____

_____

_____

2. Which body system is your brain part of?

_____

_____

What Do You Think? (p. 509)

Answer these questions in your ScienceLog now. Then later, you'll have a chance to revise your answers based on what you've learned.

Investigate! (p. 509)

3. Do you think you would have a faster reaction with the hand you write with or your other hand?

_____

_____

Section 1: The Nervous System (p. 510)

4. What do hearing a knock at the door, working a math problem, and feeling your heart pound all have in common?

_____

_____

5. Which of the following are jobs of the nervous system? (Circle all that apply.)

   a. gathering and interpreting information
   b. allowing you to speak, smell, taste, hear, and see
   c. keeping your organs working properly
   d. speeding up your heart rate during exercise

Chapter 21, continued

Two Systems Within a System (p. 510)

6. How does your nervous system act as a central command post?

_____

_____

_____

Mark each of the following statements *P* for peripheral nervous system or *C* for central nervous system.

7. _____ is made of nerves

8. _____ processes incoming and outgoing messages

9. _____ includes your brain and spinal cord

10. _____ carries information to and from all areas of your body

11. The central and peripheral nervous systems are not connected.

True or False? (Circle one.)

The Peripheral Nervous System (p. 511)

12. Specialized cells in your body that transfer messages in the form

of electrical energy are called _____ .

13. Electrical messages, called _____ , may

travel as fast 150 m/s or as slow as _____ m/s.

Match each of the terms in Column B with the correct description in Column A, and write the corresponding letter in the space provided.

Column A	Column B
_____ **14.** allows the neuron to receive information	**a.** cell body
_____ **15.** a long fiber that transmits information to other cells	**b.** dendrite
_____ **16.** contains cell organelles and a nucleus	**c.** axon

17. Some axons extend almost 1 m from

   a. your fingertips to your shoulder.

   b. your lower back to your toes.

   c. your neck to your tailbone.

   d. your wrist to your fingertip.

18. Receptors are specialized dendrites on sensory neurons that detect changes inside and outside the body. True or False? (Circle one.)

19. What are the functions of motor neurons?

_____

_____

_____

Just a Bundle of Axons (p. 512)

20. Nerves do NOT contain

    a. muscle fiber.   **c.** axons.
    b. blood vessels.   **d.** connective tissue.

21. All nerves contain the axons of sensory and motor neurons.

    True or False? (Circle one.)

The Central Nervous System (p. 513)

22. The brain is the largest organ of the central nervous system.

    True or False? (Circle one.)

Mark each of the following actions *V* for voluntary or *I* for involuntary.

23. _____ digestion

24. _____ moving your arm

25. _____ body processes that happen automatically

26. The three connected parts of the brain are the

    _____ , the _____ ,

    and the _____ .

27. What is NOT true of the cerebrum?

    a. It is the largest part of the brain.
    b. It allows you to sense things.
    c. It controls involuntary movements.
    d. It stores most memories.

28. The right hand is controlled by the _____ hemisphere of the cerebrum. (left or right)

29. Take a look at Figure 4. The right cerebral hemisphere controls activities that involve imagination and creativity.

    True or False? (Circle one.)

30. Which part of the brain keeps you from losing your balance when you stand on one foot? Explain.

_____

_____

_____

31. Which of the following functions are controlled by the part of the brain called the medulla? (Circle all that apply.)

   a. speech   **c.** involuntary breathing

   b. blood pressure   **d.** heart rate

The Spinal Cord (p. 515)

32. The rings of bone that protect your spinal cord are called

_____ .

33. Spinal cord injuries can prevent sensory information from

traveling to the _____ and motor

commands from getting to _____ nerves.

Ouch! That Hurt! (p. 516)

34. Your brain controls reflex actions. True or False? (Circle one.)

Review (p. 516)

Now that you've finished Section 1, review what you learned by answering the Review questions in your ScienceLog.

Section 2: Responding to the Environment (p. 517)

1. How do you know when someone is tapping on your shoulder if you don't see them?

_____

_____

Come to Your Senses (p. 517)

2. Sensory receptors have sensations. True or False? (Circle one.)

3. Sensory receptors in your eyes detect _____ ;

sensory receptors in your nose detect tiny _____
in the air.

Something in My Eye (p. 518)

4. Take a look at Figure 10. Why do you suppose a carrot looks orange to you?

   a. My rods see only orange light.
   b. The carrot reflects blue light.
   c. The carrot absorbs all visible light except orange light.
   d. None of the above

Choose the term in Column B that best matches the definition in Column A, and write the corresponding letter in the space provided.

Column A	Column B
____ **5.** photoreceptor needed to see color	**a.** cornea
____ **6.** opening in the eye	**b.** pupil
____ **7.** carries nerve impulses from photoreceptors	**c.** retina
____ **8.** protects the eye and allows light to enter	**d.** optic nerve
____ **9.** photoreceptor important for night vision	**e.** rod
____ **10.** light-sensitive layer in the back of the eye	**f.** cone

11. The _____ gives your eye its color and controls the amount of _____ that passes to the retina by regulating the size of the pupil.

12. How does the shape of the lens change in order to focus on an object?

_____

_____

_____

13. _____ occurs when the lens of the eye focuses light just in front of the retina instead of on the retina.

14. In Figure 12 at the bottom of page 519, corrective lenses bend light rays to correct nearsightedness or farsightedness.

   True or False? (Circle one.)

Did You "Ear" That? (p. 520)

15. When sound _____ reach your ear, you experience a _____ called hearing.

16. Put the following statements in the proper sequence to explain how we hear by writing the appropriate number in the space provided.

_____ One of the tiny ear bones vibrates against a snail-shaped organ.

_____ Inside the cochlea, vibrations create waves.

_____ Sound waves are funneled to the ear canal.

_____ Neurons convert waves into electrical impulses and send them to the brain.

_____ The eardrum vibrates against tiny bones.

Does This Suit Your Taste? (p. 521)

17. The four kinds of taste buds are salty, sweet,

_____ , and _____ .

Your Nose Knows (p. 521)

18. Why is it difficult to taste food with a stuffed nose?

_____

_____

_____

_____

_____

19. Smell receptors are located in the upper part of your nasal cavity.

True or False? (Circle one.)

20. Take a moment to read the Physical Science Connection on page 521. Is a human or a dolphin able to hear higher sounds? Explain.

_____

_____

_____

Review (p. 521)

Now that you've finished Section 2, review what you learned by answering the Review questions in your ScienceLog.

Section 3: The Endocrine System (p. 522)

1. Which of the following processes is NOT controlled by your endocrine system?

   a. fluid balance   **c.** reflex action

   b. growth   **d.** sexual development

Chemical Messengers (p. 522)

2. An endocrine _____ is a group of cells in your body that makes special chemical messengers called

   _____ .

3. What chemical messenger produces the "fight or flight" response?

   _____

   _____

Take a moment to look at Figure 17 on page 523. Choose the endocrine gland in Column B that best matches the function in Column A, and write the corresponding letter in the space provided.

Column A	Column B
_____ 4. helps your body fight disease	**a.** thyroid
_____ 5. increases the rate at which you use energy	**b.** adrenal
_____ 6. regulates blood sugar levels	**c.** testes
_____ 7. produce hormones involved in reproduction in males	**d.** pituitary
_____ 8. produce hormones involved in reproduction in females	**e.** ovaries
_____ 9. helps the body respond to stress	**f.** pancreas
_____ 10. regulates calcium levels	**g.** parathyroid
_____ 11. among other things, stimulates skeletal growth	**h.** thymus

Controlling the Controls (p. 524)

12. Special systems in your body called feedback controls tell your endocrine glands when to start and stop making hormones.

    True or False? (Circle one.)

13. Look at Figure 18 on page 524. Place the following statements in the correct order to explain the feedback control that regulates sugar. Write the appropriate number in the space provided.

_____ Glucose is absorbed into the bloodstream by the small intestine.

_____ Blood sugar levels return to normal.

_____ The pancreas releases insulin into the blood.

_____ Glucose is converted to glycogen and stored for future use.

_____ You eat again to keep your blood sugar level from falling.

_____ Insulin signals the liver to take in glucose.

_____ The pancreas stops releasing insulin.

_____ You eat a meal.

Hormone Imbalances (p. 525)

14. The pancreas produces the hormone _____. This special chemical sends a message to the cells to take in

glucose and sends a message to the _____ to store glucose.

15. How can a person with diabetes mellitus keep the glucose in the blood at a safe level?

_____

_____

_____

_____

16. Which gland produces the growth hormone?
   a. thyroid   **c.** thymus
   b. adrenals   **d.** pituitary

17. The thyroid gland can swell and form a _____

if it doesn't receive enough _____ to make the hormone thyroxine.

Review (p. 525)

Now that you've finished Section 3, review what you learned by answering the Review questions in your ScienceLog.

CHAPTER
22 DIRECTED READING WORKSHEET

Reproduction and Development

As you read Chapter 22, which begins on page 532 of your textbook, answer the following questions.

Strange but True! (p. 532)

1. What makes the tiny, hairless animal climb into its mother's pouch after it is born?

_____

_____

2. How long does a joey develop inside its mother's pouch?
  a. until it can eat solid food
  b. until its mother kicks it out of the pouch
  c. until it is ready to reproduce

What Do You Think? (p. 533)

Answer these questions in your ScienceLog now. Then later, you'll have a chance to revise your answers based on what you've learned.

Investigate! (p. 533)

3. What is being compared in this activity?

_____

_____

_____

Section 1: Animal Reproduction (p. 534)

4. Why do animals reproduce?

_____

_____

A Chip off the Old Block (p. 534)

5. When a parent has offspring that are _____ identical to itself, we call it asexual reproduction.

6. Budding occurs when a young hydra develops from a small part of the parent's body. True or False? (Circle one.)

_____

Chapter 22, continued

_____

7. Why might you get more sea stars in the ocean if you chop them up and throw them back?

_____

_____

_____

It Takes Two (p. 535)

8. Which of the following is NOT true of sexual reproduction?

    a. It usually involves two parents.

    b. Most animals reproduce this way.

    c. The offspring is genetically identical to the parent.

    d. Male and female parents produce different sex cells.

9. Sperm are sex cells produced by the _____ parent. Eggs are sex cells produced by the

_____ parent.

10. When the nuclei of an egg and a sperm cell combine, a

_____ is created.

Mark each of the following statements *True* or *False*.

11. _____ The only human cells that do not have 23 chromosomes are eggs and sperm.

12. _____ Eggs and sperm are formed by a process called meiosis.

13. _____ Each sex cell can have a different genetic combination.

14. _____ Genes are the instructions contained in the DNA.

15. A human _____ , which forms when

an egg and a sperm join, has _____ chromosomes.

16. Each zygote is able to grow into a unique individual because of

the combination of genes from both parents. True or False? (Circle one.)

Internal and External Fertilization (p. 536)

17. Which of the following are true of external fertilization? (Circle all that apply.)

   a. Sperm fertilize the eggs outside the female's body.
   b. It must take place on land.
   c. Some fishes and amphibians reproduce this way.

18. External fertilization happens when eggs and sperm join inside

   the female's body. True or False? (Circle one.)

19. Which of the following animals reproduce only by internal fertilization? (Circle all that apply.)

   a. reptiles   c. amphibians
   b. mammals   d. birds

20. How do penguins take care of their fertilized eggs?

   _____

   _____

   _____

Making Mammals (p. 537)

Mark each of the following statements *True* or *False*.

21. _____ Milk oozes from the pores of a mother monotreme.

22. _____ Marsupials lay eggs.

23. _____ Some marsupials don't have a pouch.

24. _____ Marsupials with pouches have extra bones to support the weight of their young.

25. _____ Echidnas and whales are placental mammals.

26. _____ Placental mammals nourish their young internally before birth.

27. _____ All mammals are born well-developed.

Review (p. 537)

Now that you've finished Section 1, review what you learned by answering the Review questions in your ScienceLog.

Section 2: Human Reproduction (p. 538)

1. A human offspring develops for about _____ in its mother before being born.

The Male Reproductive System (p. 538)

2. Why are sperm produced in a sac that hangs from the body?

  a. They are less likely to be crushed by internal body pressure.
  b. Normal body temperature is too warm for them to properly develop.
  c. It's easier for the body to regulate their production.
  d. The scrotum is 3 degrees warmer than body temperature.

Choose the word in Column B that best matches the description in Column A, and write the corresponding letter in the space provided.

Column A	Column B
_____ **3.** skin-covered sac that holds the testes	**a.** vas deferens
_____ **4.** temporary storage area for sperm	**b.** urethra
_____ **5.** transfers semen into the female during sexual intercourse	**c.** testes
_____ **6.** time of life when sex organs mature	**d.** scrotum
_____ **7.** tube in the penis	**e.** semen
_____ **8.** masses of tightly coiled tubes where sperm cells are produced	**f.** epididymis
_____ **9.** make sperm and testosterone	**g.** seminiferous tubules
_____ **10.** the long tube that sperm take from the storage area to the body	**h.** penis
_____ **11.** mixture of sperm and fluids	**i.** puberty

The Female Reproductive System (p. 539)

12. Which of the following is done by the female reproductive system? (Circle all that apply.)

  a. giving birth
  b. nurturing fertilized eggs
  c. producing eggs in the ovaries

13. A mature egg is almost _____ times larger than a sperm.

14. Which is the correct path for an egg beginning at ovulation?

  a. ovary wall Æ uterus Æ vagina
  b. uterus Æ fallopian tube Æ vagina
  c. ovary wall Æ fallopian tube Æ uterus
  d. ovary wall Æ uterus Æ fallopian tube

Each of the following statements is false. Change the underlined word to make each statement true, and write the correct word in the space provided.

15. The organ where a baby grows and develops is the <u>vagina</u>.

_____

16. The passageway that receives sperm during intercourse is the <u>fallopian tube</u>.

_____

17. The tube between each ovary and the uterus is called the <u>urethra</u>.

_____

18. Why does menstruation happen?

_____

_____

_____

_____

19. The menstrual cycle continues for all of a female's adult life.

True or False? (Circle one.)

Irregularities and Disorders (p. 540)

20. The two types of twins are _____ and

_____ .

21. Multiple-births are _____ .
(rare or common)

22. Why might an ectopic pregnancy be very dangerous?

_____

_____

_____

_____

_____

23. Which of the following is a cause of infertility?
(Circle all that apply.)

   a. low sperm count in men
   b. abnormal ovulation in women
   c. fallopian tubes scarred from sexually transmitted diseases

24. Sexually transmitted diseases can be passed from an infected person to an uninfected person through casual contact.

   True or False? (Circle one.)

25. The most common sexually transmitted diseases in the United States are genital herpes, chlamydia, and

   _____ .

26. AIDS can be transmitted through the sharing of needles and

   contact with infected blood. True or False? (Circle one.)

27. What parts of the reproductive systems of men and women are common sites of cancer?

   _____

   _____

   _____

Review (p. 541)

Now that you've finished Section 2, review what you learned by answering the Review questions in your ScienceLog.

Section 3: Growth and Development (p. 542)

1. There are millions of cells in your body. How did you begin your life?

   _____

   _____

A New Life (p. 542)

2. Most sperm die before reaching the egg. True or False?
(Circle one.)

3. Why is only one sperm able to get into an egg?

   _____

   _____

4. Only _____ percent of all embryos implant themselves in the mother's uterus.

Before Birth (p. 543)

5. When is a woman officially pregnant?

_____

_____

6. Which of the following are true of the placenta? (Circle all that apply.)

   a. It supplies the embryo with oxygen and nutrients from the mother's blood.
   b. It transports waste from the embryo to the mother.
   c. It contains a network of blood vessels.
   d. It helps the embryo survive.

7. The fluid-filled membrane that protects the embryo from shocks is known as the diaphragm. True or False? (Circle one.)

8. The _____ connects the embryo to the placenta.

9. In order to exchange oxygen and nutrients, the embryo's blood and the mother's blood have to mix. True or False? (Circle one)

Complete questions 10–16 after reading pages 543–545 in your textbook. Choose the time period in Column B that best matches the particular development of the fetus in Column A, and write the corresponding letter in the space provided. Time periods may be used more than once.

Column A	Column B
____ **10.** The lungs begin "practice breathing."	**a.** 1st to 2nd month
____ **11.** The embryo is developed enough to be called a fetus.	**b.** 3rd to 6th month
____ **12.** The brain begins sending signals to other parts of the body.	**c.** 7th to 9th month
____ **13.** Taste buds form on the tongue.	
____ **14.** The embryo is the size of a peanut.	
____ **15.** The fetus is able to curl its toes and hiccup.	
____ **16.** The fetus dreams.	

CHAPTER 22

__Chapter 22, continued__

Birth (p. 545)

17. The series of muscular contractions that squeeze the fetus
through the vagina at birth is known as

_____ .

18. Why do you have a navel?

_____

_____

From Birth to Death (p. 545)

19. Human infancy lasts as long as the normal life span of most

rabbits. True or False? (Circle one.)

20. Infants begin to walk as their _____
system becomes more developed.

21. Which of the following is NOT a characteristic of childhood?

    a. Your first set of teeth is replaced by permanent teeth.
    b. Your muscles become more coordinated.
    c. You grow slowly.
    d. Your intellectual abilities develop.

22. The _____ systems of young males and
females mature during puberty.

23. During puberty, boys become more muscular, the fat in their hips

increases, and their voices deepen. True or False? (Circle one.)

24. At puberty, young females begin to menstruate and their breasts

begin to enlarge. True or False? (Circle one.)

25. Which of the following are typical _early_ signs of aging?
(Circle all that apply.)

    a. increased body fat   **c.** deteriorating hearing
    b. wrinkling skin   **d.** declining athletic ability

26. How have some people been able to slow the aging process?

_____

_____

_____

Review (p. 547)

Now that you've finished Section 3, review what you learned by
answering the Review questions in your ScienceLog.